Life's Ironies: My Life on the Road Less Traveled

Life's Ironies: My Life on the Road Less Traveled

TODD KRAUSE

StoryTerrace

Text Caroline Banton, on behalf of StoryTerrace
Copyright © Todd Krause

First print April 2023

StoryTerrace

www.StoryTerrace.com

CONTENTS

INTRODUCTION

I've given a lot of thought as to why I'm still around. You see, compared to others I've talked to, and believe me, I've talked to a lot, I feel like a cat with nine lives. Early on in life, I had so many near misses that I became convinced someone up there was looking out for me. But who? And for what? I'm hardly special.

Near misses weren't the only thing that made me contemplate my mortality and reason for being; my health has been a constant challenge ever since I was a small child. I have suffered from chronic illness all my life, and as others in similar situations can attest, it's debilitating and scary.

As an adult, I worked in finance. Amazingly, it proved to be an experience I never imagined someone like me would have. The people I worked with influenced me and opened my eyes to a world of possibilities despite my hindrances. I learned how to navigate a path to relative financial freedom from a place of meager living. But more importantly, I think I am beginning to finally understand what I was really meant for.

I believe that anyone can succeed in a non-traditional way by following non-traditional paths. Also, only *YOU* can define what success is to you and how you arrive there. For most of my life, I didn't know what success really was or what it felt like. I thought I did, and when I reached the higher echelons of banking and finance, it was a huge disappointment. It wasn't until later, and after a series of setbacks and a lifelong struggle with my health, that I finally figured it out.

Here's my story.

1. THE CALL

One early Wednesday evening in January 2022, around 5:30 p.m., I received an email from the chief operating officer of The Cleaning Authority, one of 14 brands owned by The Authority Brands, a home service franchise company. I was the owner and operator of a local office, one of the hundreds of individually owned offices across these brands, which provides home and business cleaning services. The COO oversaw all of the Cleaning Authority brand's franchise operations.

I read the email with concern. The COO wanted me to join her on a Microsoft Teams call at 8:45 a.m. the following day. Call me a Debbie downer, but when the corporate COO schedules a meeting first thing the following day, it's rarely good news.

Oh crap, I thought as my stomach did a 360. *What did we do?* I went through a whole checklist of reasons for her to call a meeting. *Did we break something? Steal something? Offend a client?*

I was so stunned that I neglected to check the invite to see who else was to attend the meeting. That was lucky because had I noticed the four other senior VPs cc'd on the invite, I would have hyperventilated all night. As it was, I retired to bed with a prayer. A stiff Scotch would have been appropriate, but I don't drink.

2. NEAR MISSES AND GUARDIAN ANGELS

"I'm convinced that while some people have a guardian angel, God found it necessary to give me a team of them, and I've kept them eternally busy."

I've had many near misses in my life, and as I grew older, my seeming ability to walk away unscathed from accidents made me wonder if I was here for a higher purpose. I have always been a religious and spiritual person, so I was open to the idea that a higher power was looking out for me, but I could never figure out why.

I grew up in Hebron, Wisconsin, a small, unincorporated town eight miles east of Fort Atkinson, which is south of I91 about halfway between Madison and Milwaukee. My maternal and paternal grandparents all emigrated from Germany as small children before World War I to this area of southeastern Wisconsin. My parents were cold and regimented, which I now realize handicapped me in some ways in my relationships with others.

My parents dated in high school in Watertown, Wisconsin. After graduation, my father purchased his first bulk milk delivery route while he and my mother threw together a hastily planned marriage. They were married December 27th, 1958, in a simple ceremony in church in front of a small group of friends and relatives. Immediately after that, and nearly every day for many years, my father picked up milk from local farms and delivered it to the dairy in Whitewater.

My father was also a national guard reservist, and a couple of years after my parents were married, he was called to active duty. My parents were told it was due to the Berlin crisis that occurred around 1961. Oddly, his unit was sent out west to Yakima, Washington. Before his departure, he dutifully sold the milk route and headed west to help defend Berlin.

As my father's active duty ended, my mother was pregnant. My parents packed up again and drove back to southeastern Wisconsin through Montana, the Dakotas, and across Minnesota.

Back home, my parents rented an old, slightly dilapidated farmhouse on Highway D, south of Helenville. It was not a place of beauty by any means. The floors in each room sagged noticeably, and I remember my toys rolling toward the center of the room whenever I played on the floor. We entered the home through a large, screened-in porch that doubled as our laundry room. The laundry equipment was an old electric washing machine with hand-rollers for wringing out clothes above the washing machine wash tub. Clotheslines for drying damp clothes crisscrossed overhead on the porch. During the colder months, the clotheslines stretched across the kitchen. Anyone visiting let themselves into the screened porch, crossed through the laundry area, and knocked at the kitchen door.

The kitchen had two sets of stairs, one set of stairs led down to the dark cement cellar, and next to those were the stairs up to the second floor, the bedrooms, and the main bathroom. We used the second floor for sleeping and bathing only; back then, nobody lived in their bedrooms the way we do today. We lived primarily in the large kitchen, where we ate at the dining table. There was a large living room adjacent to the kitchen where we had an old black and white television.

The first of my mishaps occurred in that aged farmhouse.

My mother was washing dishes at the kitchen sink one day, and I was a baby crawling around under her feet. Apparently, she was washing a large butcher's knife when it slipped from her hands and dropped, narrowly missing me as it clattered to the floor. My mother needed a moment.

Another incident occurred on a cold, Wisconsin winter's day. I was a toddler, and my mother had sent me outside to play in the snow. The day was bright and sunny but intensely cold, and the fun white stuff soon lost its appeal. I became worried and didn't know what to do with myself outside and alone.

I wandered around the yard, looked at snow-covered things, jumped in the drifts, and began to feel even colder. When I went to the porch screen door to let myself into the house, the door handle came off in my hand. I tried desperately to open the door by grabbing the screw sticking out where the handle had been a moment before. I tried with and without my mittens, but nothing worked. I pounded on the door and shouted for my mother, but there was no response to my urgent calls. I couldn't understand why she didn't come for me and why I was left outside alone in the freezing cold. I laid down on the cement steps and started to cry. I have no idea how long I lay there.

The next thing I remember is sitting on my mother's lap with my feet dangling over the edge of the bathtub in the second-floor bathroom as she pulled my cold, wet clothes and boots off and dropped them into the tub in a pile. She gave me a warm bath to reheat me. I remember this episode vividly. That day had a profound effect on me. It was the beginning of the loss of childhood innocence. I lost trust in people and realized that anyone could prove undependable and unreliable.

We also survived two tornados in that ramshackle home. The first time, my mother and maternal grandmother were baking cookies in the kitchen. I was playing with toys under the table unperturbed as the winds picked up to gale force around us. My mother and grandmother said they could hear the tornado roar as it passed by and ripped roofs off barns across the road. They recall looking at each other during the storm, thinking, what should we do? For some reason, they didn't move to the cellar for safety. I continued playing beneath the table while they carried on making cookies. Keep calm and carry on, I suppose. Luckily, we did.

The second tornado ripped through on a summer's afternoon. My mother and I were alone in the house. She was working in the kitchen, and I was playing with my toys in front of the doors to the stairs as the skies darkened and the winds raged. This time my mother scooped me up and carried me through the door to the stairs leading down to the cellar. We stood on a step about halfway down. My mother listened as the tornado roared past. Once again, we were unscathed.

Over the next six or seven years, there were other times when I had near misses that could have turned out much worse. When I was around 10 years old, we had moved to a new house that my parents built on Lower Hebron Road. I had some friends over one day, and we were running around in the basement. For some reason, there was a piece of plate glass lying on the table, and the corner edge was sticking out. I ran past it, and it sliced into my elbow. My mother took me to the bathroom, washed it up, and taped it shut with some medical tape. We were a family that only went to the doctor when we absolutely had to.

* * *

I think a guardian angel must have played a role in another episode a year or so later, too. When I was around 11, I started to really enjoy trap shooting. I used my grandfather's break-action 20-gauge shotgun that he had used for hunting. My mother operated the clay pigeon throwers for me. They were manual—the spring-loaded arm had to be pulled back until it latched and to allow the loading of the clay pigeon. When I was ready, my mother would yank a little cord that released the arm, and the thrower would fling the clay disc out. It had adjustable angles allowing us to change how high, low, left, or right the clay disc flew, making the target move in many different directions.

I had used my grandfather's gun many times, but one day, it surprised me. It fired two or three times before I was ready. In the process of firing, it slid through my hands, and by the time

I could grab a hold of it, I was holding the barrel, not the stock. I assumed I was somehow bumping the trigger before I was ready. The next time I used the gun, the same thing happened, only the hammer on the gun ripped through my shirt and my chest. It had one of those hammers that were sharp at the back and that you cocked back with your thumb. Then, the hammer slammed forward when you pulled the trigger and fired the shell. The sharp edge of the hammer came down and ripped through my shirt and chest.

I realized at this point that I was not bumping the trigger as I had initially thought, but the gun was malfunctioning. Something was failing inside this gun and not keeping the hammer cocked. The gun was firing before I could position it against my shoulder. Every time it fired, it slid through my hands until I grabbed it by the barrel. It was my grandfather's gun, so I wanted to keep it, but the gunsmith said it was not repairable, because the parts were no longer available. He removed the firing pin so it couldn't be used again, and for several years we hung it on the wall in the basement. It was a reminder to me of my "near misses," and that I needed to preserve what was left of my nine lives.

* * *

We took camping trips as a family. My parents had a 1967 Chevy Impala—white on the outside with a red vinyl interior. In those early days, we packed the trunk and pulled a trailer behind with our camping gear. My dad had rigged up some supports and used a tarp to make a roof over the work trailer.

My parents loved going to Devil's Lake State Park, 30 to 40 miles northwest of Madison, Wisconsin. It's a spring-fed lake surrounded by 400 to 600-foot bluffs with boulder fields at the base. My brother and I loved to hike on the trails, swim in the lake, climb around in the boulder fields, and then go up on the bluffs. One trip when I was around 10 or so, my friend Jim Nimmer came along with us.

Jim and I explored a different bluff every day. There was the east bluff, the north bluff, and the south bluff surrounding the lake. One evening, we decided to climb up the south bluff to watch the sunset. We had flashlights so we could descend safely to the campground along the trails. We were climbing up the bluff with flashlights shoved in our rear pockets when I reached up for a ledge. It was covered with pine needles, and I didn't have a good grip. My hand slipped, and I fell backward off the face of the bluff. They say that your life flashes before your eyes in such moments, but that wasn't the case for me. I just froze and thought, Oh shit. I'm falling. I wonder how that happened?

I landed on my back partway down. The trunk of a tree that was growing out from the side of the bluff stopped my fall and saved me from falling to the base of the bluff where there was nothing but large boulders and rocks.

I was left stunned by that event.

* * *

At this point in my life, I didn't need much more proof that either I was extremely lucky or that someone somewhere was saving me for something. Still, the evidence kept piling up.

When I turned 16, I wasn't in much of a hurry to drive, as I was interested in other things. However, I did get my license, and one Saturday, December afternoon, I was driving home after roller-skating on a gray, overcast, cold, and damp winter's day. I remember the sun was low in the sky, and I went into a corner a bit too fast and hit black ice. The car slid out of control, skidding back and forth across the road. I was in the oncoming lane for a moment, headed right toward a car coming my way. At the last minute, I swerved back into my lane, but the momentum kept the Impala going off the right side of the road, and I plowed sideways through 300 feet of fence. The car slid along the fence, knocking down posts, with barbed wire sawing through the body panels.

When my car finally stopped, the other car backed up to give me a lift to the farmhouse so I could ask for help to pull the Impala out of the ditch. Interestingly, it was an old classmate of mine from grade school, Nina. She was with her boyfriend. I pondered what the aftermath of a head-on collision with me would have looked like.

The couple drove me up to the farmhouse where the farmer agreed to help me. He pulled my car out of the ditch, up to the farmhouse, and helped me remove the barbed wire from the body panels. He looked at the car and what was left of his fence at the accident scene.

"Well," he said, "You can pay me for the fence, or you can come back in the spring and remove the rest of it."

I didn't have a whole lot of money, so I said, "I'll see you in the spring."

In early April, it warmed up, and we had a reasonably nice day. I went back to the scene, removed the rest of the fence posts, neatly coiled and stacked all the barbed wire, and settled my debts with the farmer.

* * *

If a Chevy Impala had caused me some headaches, motorcycles were worse. I owned a Kawasaki 385 that I bought from a neighbor, a blacksmith who did specialized metalwork and didn't want the Kawasaki anymore.

After I'd owned it a while, I was coming home from a friend's house. It had rained, and I dumped it over right in front of a semi. I slid through the intersection across the slick road. It was like some James Bond movie, only less entertaining. I picked up the bike and kept going. I was equally dazed by both the fall and the realization that I had, once again, evaded death.

One time I was riding without a helmet, listening for engine noise. I thought Oh, now I hear it, and I looked down. Just turning my head slightly was enough for the wind to catch my glasses and pull them off my face. I could see them in the rearview mirror, spinning on the pavement behind me. They never broke. The lenses weren't even scratched. I felt like Harry Potter.

There were plenty of times I dumped the bike over, because I hit everything from loose gravel to wet, slick leaves, so at a certain point, I didn't have much desire to own a motorcycle again.

These experiences are just some of the reasons I started to wonder how in the world I could be so lucky so often. I might not be most people's favorite in my earthly environment, but somebody up there liked me. Why exactly?

3. GROWING UP ... A CIRCUS EXPERIENCE

"*Oh Todd. It can't be that bad. You're making a mountain out of a molehill.*"

My Kindergarten days were a shock to my system because I hadn't learned how to interact with other children. In mid-March 1967, we moved into a new house my parents had built. It was a three-bedroom ranch with one and a half baths, a full basement, and a two-car garage. The house sat on a five-acre wooded lot of mostly mature oak trees.

On the other side of the road and down a bit was an old farm owned by Hallie and Eva Wintermute. The Wintermutes were an old circus family. The Circus Museum in Baraboo, Wisconsin, still has pictures and exhibits with models based on their circus. Hallie and Eva Wintermute were an older couple who would tell us stories about the circus back in its day.

I remember the house had a hand pump over a trough for a sink in the kitchen and an outhouse in the back. It didn't even have indoor plumbing or heating, but it did have electricity for lights.

The Wintermutes never had much money, but every Christmas they gave my brother and I one dollar each and my dad a small bottle of Mogen David wine. My brother and I used to love to go over to the Wintermutes' to play. Soon, though, I was to enter another circus environment and one that offered a quite different Big Top experience.

***

I went to parochial schools, where the administration was carried out by the principal, the administrative staff, and the teachers. However, some of the religion classes and all of the confirmation classes were taught by pastors, who certainly did not practice what they preached, and nor did the principal and teachers.

Before I attended Kindergarten, I used to watch the school bus go by and pick up children. I watched the children board the bus with envy, because I longed for company. However, when it came time to start Kindergarten, I was terrified. I hadn't been around anybody other than my younger brother. The first day of Kindergarten, my mother had to physically lift me up and put me on the bus to St. Paul's Lutheran in Fort Atkinson.

The pastors taught various religion classes, especially at the higher grades—fifth, sixth, seventh, and eighth—as we were approaching confirmation. Bullying was rife at the school, and the administrators, teachers, and the pastors ignored what went on in front of them, and in some cases they acted as bullies themselves. As a child, this was incredibly confusing and disappointing. However, there is an upside to most things in life. In my case, it knocked the innocence out of me, and I gained a sense of independence and determination.

I largely enjoyed Kindergarten, first, and second grade. However, in second grade, my friend Jim Nimmer and I were goofing around during choir rehearsal one day. The teacher called us out in front of everybody and criticized us for our behavior. I'm sure we deserved it, but I felt shamed. In that moment, a switch flipped for me, and I never felt like singing again.

This shaming of students in front of their peers was a pattern of behavior among the teachers and pastors in the parochial school system. It had damaging effects on me, and, I suspect, many other children. In fourth grade, I initially respected and liked a teacher who supervised our softball and was very fair. He insisted everybody could play, not just the best kids. But then, somewhere near the end of the year, I said or did something in the lunchroom—I don't know what it was. Something happened around the trash cans, where we scraped the food remains off the plates, and it set him off. He grabbed me by the neck in front of everyone and lifted me into the air. My feet were dangling, and I was eyeball to eyeball with him, completely powerless. At that moment, my respect for him evaporated.

The disciplinary style of the teachers verged on abusive if it wasn't outright abuse. The hypocrisy of what they taught us and how they treated us severely shook my faith and desire to be a part of the church.

Things were no better in fifth grade. A teacher called Mr. Ottenbacher, who had a particularly strange approach to discipline, made a friend and I stand in the hallway with our feet two feet away from the wall. We had to lean our forehead against the concrete cinder block wall that was painted over with textured paint. My friend started to cry because it hurt so much.

The culture of cruelty rubbed off on the older kids, and this was particularly evident on the school buses at the end of the day. The teachers were also the bus drivers, and they didn't come out to the buses until the buses were full. Day after day, the big kids on the bus grabbed us by our coats, picked us up, and slammed us down in our seats.

From fifth to seventh grade, I was in band. I was picked on between the time school let out as all of us were gathering in the band room until the time when the band instructor arrived. There was one very physically large boy who played the tuba and would pick me up and slam me down in my chair each time, just like the boys on the bus would do. One day, I'd finally just had enough. I had these heavy shoes on with thick lug soles, and I kicked him hard in the groin. He danced and hopped around in pain for a while afterward.

He completely left me alone after that.

The teachers did nothing about the bullying, and I complained bitterly to my parents about it.

"Oh, it can't be as bad as that," my parents said. "You're making a mountain out of a molehill. You need to develop a thicker skin."

The thing about abuse is that victims feel powerless, and that's even more true when you ask others for help, and they dismiss what you say.

When not in the confines of school, we were typical kids doing kid things. From sixth to eighth grade, we found ways to drink alcohol at sleepovers. We scraped our money together, gave 20 bucks to a friend's older brother, and asked them to go to the liquor store for us. We asked them to hide whatever they had bought under the bushes in front of the house and keep the rest of the money. My friend's parents were forever telling us to quiet down as we were sneaking sips of beer, laughing, being silly, and letting loose.

* * *

I did have a tight group of friends for a while starting in grade school. We called ourselves The Four Musketeers. We were all nerdy types, not particularly gifted when it came to sports, and we tended to gravitate toward all things science. We bonded around science because we were mostly ostracized by the popular kids and always picked last when it came time to be divided up into teams in gym class and on the playground.

Instead of playing sports, the Four Musketeers dug around in the dusty sections of the library where there were books on physics, chemistry, and biology. We bought supplies for science experiments from a company called NASCO in Fort Atkinson. The company also supplied the schools' biology, chemistry, and physics departments with equipment and supplies.

We could walk into the store and buy beakers, test tubes, Bunsen burners, or whatever we needed. We could say, "I want a pound of potassium nitrate," or "I want a pound of pure ground sulfur" and they sold it to us.

Independently, I particularly enjoyed building model rockets that I bought from a company called Estes. One of the rockets I built was a model of the Saturn V that was over three feet tall. I painted it with black and white panels to resemble the Saturn V used in the Apollo launches to carry the astronauts to the moon. However, the store sold me the wrong type of engine. The company sold me a booster engine, which has a very hot back blast to ignite the rocket engines in the next stage. In this case, there weren't secondary engines in the rocket to ignite, and the hot back blast of the booster engines melted the plastic model. I cut out the melted sections, glued the tail section and the nose cone sections together, and tested it following the instructions in a book on model rocketry. The book explained how to test a model rocket to see if it will fly stably. Everything indicated it would, so I put it on the little launchpad and launched it.

The next few minutes were like a cartoon. The rocket flew around in crazy eights in the air while everyone around was ducking and diving. It carried on until the engine burned itself out, and then it just plopped on the ground in the backyard. We were all a bit speechless after that episode.

As my love for science deepened, I found myself fascinated by osteology. At first I tried to experiment a bit on my own by getting a cow head from the local slaughterhouse, and cleaning it up by boiling away the flesh. But as I studied, I got to know someone who worked at NASCO and found out that one of his tasks was to collect the bones from animal carcasses by dissolving the flesh in a solution. Then, he reconstructed the bones into skeletons to sell to the biology departments of schools and they were displayed in their science classrooms. His method seemed much more efficient (scientific?) than mine, and I felt like there was a lot that I could learn from him, so we became good friends. He showed me a whole science lab that he had built in a backyard storage shed that was probably roughly 8x10 feet. It was the type of shed that most people used to store their lawnmower and bicycles. He wanted to sell his science lab and supplies, so he let me purchase it all for around $10 and on the condition that I came to pick everything up and haul it away.

I also set up a lab in the basement where I remember having a test tube full of mercury, which was interesting. I was amazed how it stuck together when I poured it onto a flat surface.

And of course, there were fireworks. I think all boys must have a fireworks story. I remember at one point, we had some fireworks and were playing around. I lit a firecracker and threw it in the old drum that we used to burn trash. I waited for it to go off, but it didn't. *That's odd*, I thought, *I wonder what's going on?* So, I walked up and peeked in the trash barrel. At that moment, it went off, practically in my face. I wasn't hurt; my face just turned a bit black.

When I reached fifth or sixth grade, our teachers considered our close group of nerdy friends, the Four Musketeers, a clique. The teachers told us we needed to make other friends, and they started criticizing us and interfering. By seventh going into eighth grade, the teachers had succeeded in driving a wedge between us, and we had a falling out. That was the end of our science sanctuary, our bond, and the Four Musketeers.

* * *

The bullying continued nonstop in high school. People do a lot of growing in their final years of high school, so much so that seniors are huge in comparison to freshmen and significantly stronger too. My friend Steve retaliated against the bullies by supergluing their lockers shut. Each time, after he was bullied, we could hear the janitor with a hammer and chisel trying to pry the bully's locker open. The noise could be heard throughout the school, the classrooms, and the study halls. *OK*, I'd think. *Someone's been messing with Steve again.*

Still though, I hated the bullying less than I did the hypocrisy. We were taught Bible messages about loving others and caring for their wellbeing, but then the teachers turned a blind eye to the violence and cruelty that occurred daily. I could never reconcile how they could preach high moral standards and then turn around and let this behavior continue.

Early on in my freshman year at Lakeside Lutheran High, Pastor Stuebs told our class a riddle and said if we could give him an answer, we could earn extra credit. My friend Dave and I were being tutored in Spanish at the time and instead of paying attention in our tutoring session that day, we were joking about the riddle. More accidentally than anything else, we stumbled on the answer. We were thrilled and went to Pastor Stuebs to claim our extra credit.

He wouldn't give it to us. He accused us of getting the answer from upperclassmen who already knew the riddle. I'll admit that we had tried, but the upperclassmen all refused to help us. We discovered the answer to the riddle through our own efforts. That marked the beginning of a downward spiral in the relationship between Pastor Stuebs and I.

I disagreed with Pastor Stuebs on many things. One such subject was what happens when you die, and is there an afterlife? He assumed a stance whereby he claimed that people died, and that was that. You only live once.

"Yes," I said to him. "However, God is the Almighty and the all-powerful. And if God wants somebody to come back from the dead, he certainly could make that happen."

Everyone wants to be respected as they grow up, and it felt like Pastor Stuebs wasn't taking me seriously. As time went by, our relationship deteriorated beyond repair, and by the time I left high school, we didn't speak much anymore. This culminated, in my senior year, when Pastor Stuebs kicked me out of his religion class. He wouldn't give me the grade that I needed to graduate, so my parents came to the school and talked to him. My parents and Pastor Stuebs worked out a compromise whereby I would do the homework for the course in a study hall but not attend the class in person.

Most times, it felt like I was all alone. No one ever seemed to believe me when I told them about the unreasonable treatment at school. However, I did sense some catharsis about 12 years later when someone from my high school class contacted my parents because they were arranging a class reunion and were trying to reach me. Somehow, this person and my parents began to talk about our experiences at Lakeside Lutheran High School. My parents listened as she told them the same things I had tried to tell them in my youth, things they had ignored or had told me I was exaggerating or making a mountain out of a molehill.

This time, because they were hearing it from somebody else, they changed their tune from "Oh! It couldn't be that bad" to "If only we'd known." I remember thinking, *where were you when I needed you? Why didn't you believe me when I tried to tell you what was happening? You had to hear it from somebody else before you finally believed me.*

* * *

There was a brighter side to high school. I had two trips at the tail end of my junior year, the first was to Spain for two weeks in April, and the second was to the Grand Canyon.

I was the only one from my school to go to Spain. After my parents drove me to O'Hare Airport in Chicago, I flew to New York City and then to Madrid with a group of students from other schools. From there, we traveled to the Valencia area, where everybody from the tour group dispersed to their respective host families for a few days. Then, we reconvened and worked our way back across southern Spain.

I remember driving with my host family in their French Citroen. I was sitting in the passenger side rear seat. I remember looking out the window and thinking, *Wow, those trees and telephone poles are flying by really fast.* I leaned forward to look over the shoulder of the driver, and the speedometer said 180 kilometers an hour. I was right, *fast.*

In those days, Spain had no legal drinking age. We were high schoolers, but we went to bars, nightclubs, and pubs. We could just walk into any establishment and order liquor if we wanted to. The drinking that I'd started in grade school was becoming a regular part of my life by my late high school years.

The Spanish night clubs were always on the lower level of buildings, down narrow stairs, and through a hallway to the area where the actual club occupied in the vast space that opened up underneath the building. Everybody smoked cigarettes, and the area was so thick with smoke, we could hardly see where we were walking.

The second trip was to the Grand Canyon at the end of my junior year and was sponsored by a couple of teachers, Mr. Bode and Mr. Adickes. These two teachers taught the Creation Science class, which was a very popular class. The premise of the subject was that science does not necessarily disagree with Bible stories, such as the Great Flood, and Mr. Bode and Mr. Adickes espoused that scientific evidence exists of a great flooding event in rock formations.

We traveled in school buses and vans to the Grand Canyon from Lake Mills, Wisconsin. We drove through Colorado, Arizona, New Mexico, and Utah, and back. It was a lot of driving. School buses have 11 rows and a total of 22 seats. Each person had a full bench seat to themselves, but it wasn't the comfiest of journeys.

We quickly learned that the buses had auxiliary gas tanks that enabled a bus to go quite a distance before they had to stop to refuel. We had many miles to cover, and we were bored. We looked out the windows as we drove, drinking water, juice, or Coke, but the drivers only wanted to stop when they needed gas, which was every six or seven hours. I discovered the limit of the fluids I could take in before I had to use the restroom. You could find yourself in a whole world of hurt waiting for them to stop again if you didn't limit your fluid intake.

We visited Rocky Mountain National Park and Mesa Verde National Park in Colorado. We climbed up Half Mountain and ate a packed lunch at the top. Even though it was late May or early June, there was snow on the mountaintop and along the trails. On the way down, we skied down the mountain in our hiking boots, and what took hours to climb up took all of about 15 or 20 minutes to descend.

We had three days of hiking through the Grand Canyon. We started on the north rim, which was bitterly cold the night before we hiked into the canyon, even though it was June. We were at a reasonably high elevation on the north rim. Even in late springtime, it can be frigid at night. We hiked down a side canyon, the Angel Bright Falls canyon, and across the Colorado River, camped at Phantom Ranch, and then ascended the rest of Angel Bright Falls canyon on the other side of the Colorado River. It was hot when we got down in the canyon, and the sun beat down on us.

The canyon is as massive as its name implies. While hiking, the requirement on the narrow trails was that we hikers stand on the outside edge of the trail and let mules and horses pass on the inside, so they didn't spook and fall into the canyon. At one point, three or four of us from the group were standing on the outside edge of the trail as a mule train passed. We looked over our shoulders down into the canyon below, thinking, *Whew, that's a long way down.* One of my classmates said, "I wouldn't want to be riding a retarded mule," as we gazed down into the vast depths of the canyon.

When the sun went down, a pitch blackness descended immediately in the canyon as if someone had turned the lights out; it was that sudden. We slept in the open on the ground. I laid on top of my sleeping bag. It was so hot down in the canyon.

On our last day, I'd had enough of everyone else and having to do everything together. I wanted to hike out of the canyon early and be on top of the south rim to watch the sunrise. I figured that if I left at three in the morning, I could make it up to the top of the south rim for the sunrise. There was considerable discussion—the teachers wouldn't let me leave that early. So, we compromised. I could leave at 5:00 a.m. I saw the sunrise when I was about halfway up, and it was magnificent.

I was one of the first to the top of the south rim of the canyon. I was also one of the first into the bus to grab clean clothes and head for the showers at the top. A few others who had also left early followed close behind. Hiking the Grand Canyon leaves you very sweaty and grimy from tramping around in the canyon, so I was looking forward to washing a layer or two off. I had to watch my time closely in the shower. You put 50 cents into the coin in the slot in the showers, and the showers gave you five minutes of water. I didn't have much money with me and thought, *I've got to maximize my usage here, I don't want to be lathered up and run out of water.*

The Grand Canyon marked the end of my school trips. At the tail end of the trip, we visited Big Sur in Phoenix, a massive water park with a wave generator that makes waves ranging from five to eight feet high. It was a fun day, apart from the Phoenix sun, which was merciless. My friend Steve was so severely sunburned that we had to stop at a hospital on the way back so he could receive medical attention. He had second-degree burns and giant blisters all over his back.

It was a long drive back to Wisconsin from Arizona. Several teachers and adults rotated driving shifts and slept in the support vans when they weren't driving. As we crossed the Texas Panhandle, the drivers asked if one of us could stay up with them in the middle of the night and talk to them to keep them alert. I took a turn sitting up front with the driver late that night. I sat on top of a cooler next to the driver. The area was so flat; it struck me how far into the distance you could see the headlights of oncoming traffic, and it seemed to take forever until we met and passed each other.

I remember thinking that our closing speed—the total of our two speeds as we came toward each other across the desert—had to be 110 or 120 miles per hour. We were going 55 or 60 miles an hour toward them, and the other car was traveling at 55 or 60 miles an hour toward us. I waited and waited until finally the car passed us heading the other way. I was amazed at the distances I could see across the Texas Panhandle.

As a young adult processing all the newness of life, including social and educational experiences, I didn't recognize it at the time, but there was something constantly gnawing away at the back of my mind. I was constantly tired and often suffered from sinus infections, allergies, and bronchitis. This had been the case since I was a small child, so I had become quite an expert at burying my thoughts on the subject. By the time I reached second and third grade, I had more than a niggling suspicion that I was not quite like my peers. They could all run faster, and throw harder, and I was always tired with no stamina. My health was to become a drag to the point where many of the "conventional" paths in life would either be unavailable to me or unsuitable.

4. UNCONVENTIONAL PATHS

My parents did not go to college, and we were never the warm, chatty type of family. My parents were not in a position to advise or counsel me on my choices, and I did much of what I did by trial and error. I then learned from my errors and tried again. After high school, I realized that whatever I was going to achieve in life, I would have to step out on my own and do it without guidance. If something didn't work out, I'd just have to find another path to get to where I wanted to go.

I started my search for a university by looking at all the schools that seemed glamorous and in warm places, such as California, Florida, and Arizona. It wasn't long before I became more realistic and narrowed my search down. There were perfectly good and cheaper schools not far from home, and I could buy a coat.

I applied to five schools, four in Wisconsin and Northwestern in Chicago, Illinois. The only time Northwestern ever showed any interest in me was long after I received both of my master's degrees and long after I had entered the world of work and had been promoted a number of times. However, as I was considering where to go for my undergraduate degree, Northwestern wouldn't give me the time of day.

The University of Wisconsin at Milwaukee accepted me, as did the University of Wisconsin at Platteville and Marquette

University. I knew I didn't want to attend the University of Wisconsin, Madison. It had over 50,000 students, and I feared I would be lost in the crowd. So, I picked Marquette University in the heart of downtown Milwaukee, which seemed much more civilized with 8,000 undergraduates and 6,000 graduate students. I was the third person in the history of my high school to attend Marquette.

I knew my interests were likely to take me toward working and living in a large city, so I thought it a good idea to attend school in a large city to see how I fared. Marquette University is in the middle of Milwaukee. Marquette itself is located in a fringe area sandwiched between diverse inner-city areas. Economically challenged African American neighborhoods were north of campus, and south of the campus was an industrial area where all the freight traffic and trains moved through. Further south were also the economically challenged Latino neighborhoods. To the east, along the lakefront were wealthy and primarily white areas. To the west were middle-class suburban areas. The city is very segregated.

It was not uncommon to be chased on the way to class by a street person who was angry because we could afford expensive tuition at Marquette while they struggled to figure out where their next meal was coming from. Most women students would not walk home from class to their dorms or apartments alone because of this.

From August 1981 to December 1985, I attended Marquette University. During my junior and senior years, I lived in Mashuda Hall, an old Holiday Inn at 20th and Wisconsin Avenue. The noteworthy thing about that building was that many years earlier, the Beatles had stayed there when they performed in Milwaukee. The school had only a few dormitory buildings when I was there, and the student housing was mainly in old hotels. The good part about that was every room had a bathroom, so we didn't have to walk down the hall to communal bathrooms and showers.

I turned 18 before attending Marquette and already had developed a pretty good drinking habit. Some of us went off the deep end indulging in alcohol at Marquette, however, and the early-80s college scene didn't help one bit. Milwaukee had a bar on every street corner, it seemed, and alcohol was our primary recreational activity. We went to happy hours where we could often buy tap beers for 10 cents each. Somebody in our group would grab a table and give the bartender $10 or $15 for tap beers, and by the time everybody arrived, the table would be lined with row after row of 10-cent tap beers. During other specials, we could buy little seven-ounce bottles of beer —I haven't seen those bottles in years. They had a distinctive shape and were called "bullets." On Tuesday nights, we could buy three bullets for a buck. Friends and I would take a chessboard with us to the bar, plunk it down on the bar, and drink bullets all night.

I met my wife, Molly, around this time. I vividly remember the first time I saw her, or at least became aware of her. It was at the start of my junior year on the first day of a required theology class. I noticed Molly because, on the first day of class, she walked in wearing a straw cowboy hat with a red bandana tied around the hat and a yellow sweatshirt with the sleeves ripped off. Her sweatshirt said "angel" on one side and "slave" on the other. As the teacher, who was a priest, began introducing himself and the course to everyone there, Molly stuck her hand in the air.

"Yes?" asked the teacher.

"Are we getting out early?" She asked.

He ignored the question and continued introducing himself. She stuck her hand up again, and he said, "Yes?"

"You didn't answer my question."

He replied dryly, "I thought I did."

The class let out about two or three minutes early. As we were leaving, the teacher said to Molly, "See, you're getting out early."

I was intrigued.

At the time, I lived on the fifth floor of Mashuda Hall, which was co-ed—one wing for women, one wing for men. Quite by accident, I wandered down the women's wing to one of the women's rooms, where I knew some people, and found Molly lying flat on their floor. We had a brief exchange.

I had liquor in my room, and I invited Molly to my room for a drink. She accepted, much to my delight. My favorite drink at the time was a gimlet, which is a rum and lime concoction. She drank part of a drink with me but didn't finish it. I later learned that she was suffering from an ulcer, and the gimlet wasn't settling with her very well.

Molly and I initially started going as part of a group of six or eight friends headed to the bars. We got to know each other and compared notes. It turned out that we'd been in multiple classes together, and I remembered her from some. One class stood out in my mind. It was a freshman math course that was held in a gigantic hall with room for what seemed like 500 students. I sat way up in the back, because I was constantly tired. She sat down in the front so she could see the board. I remembered that she had the school newspaper open, and the professor yelled at her to put it away.

Molly had transferred from a small private women's university in Columbia, Missouri, to Marquette for her junior year. She was from Winnetka, Illinois, a wealthy northern suburb of Chicago, and her father was a corporate executive. He had been the president of Leonard Construction, the construction arm for Monsanto at the time. She was dating the son of some high-powered Chicago lawyer when I met her. Her boyfriend's name was Chris, and he attended a university in Michigan.

I continued going out with this group to the bars more and more. And even when the whole group wasn't headed to the bars, Molly and I spent time together, mainly visiting various bars. Still, as long as Chris was in her life, it slowed down the development of our relationship, allowing a friendship to develop first.

The summer between junior and senior year, Molly took summer classes while I worked for the Fort Atkinson Park district about 45 to 50 miles west of Milwaukee. After I got off work on Fridays, I drove into Milwaukee to meet Molly and the rest of the group. After a night out, I stayed at her place a few times. Once or twice, it was awkward. Her boyfriend, Chris, showed up at the last minute, so I was shuffled out to one of her girlfriend's apartments until he left town.

I didn't see Chris as a good suitor for Molly. He didn't treat her particularly well, and I knew that all I had to do was be patient until she finally got sick of him and told him to go away. So, I was willing to lay low in her friend's place at a moment's notice and be supportive of her. I was there for her and helped her with her studies. All the while, I watched as Chris made mistake after mistake. Then, when he was finally out of the picture, we started dating more seriously.

Molly and I frequented the Harp & Shamrock—a seedy bar in a questionable neighborhood. We felt safe, though, because the owner kept his gigantic German Shepherd behind the bar. Anytime somebody caused trouble, the bartender would command the dog to come flying over the bar and end the dispute. If you were in with the "in-crowd," though, the dog left you alone. The bartender's name was Danny. He was an alcoholic. Even while working behind the bar, he drank as much as everybody else. He was well-versed in literature, and every time we entered the bar, he'd give us an improvised line or two from the poet Robert W. Service.

"A bunch of boys were whooping it up at the Malamute saloon when Molly McGee and entourage."

So, she was Molly McGee, and I was "entourage." I wasn't sure how I felt about that.

Showing up at the Harp & Shamrock around 10:00 p.m., having a few cocktails, and watching *M*A*S*H* reruns became a ritual for us. Hangovers were never limited to weekends. Weekdays were fair game too, and we were progressively drinking more nights a week. It started as Friday and Saturday nights, then it became Friday, Saturday, and Sunday. Soon it became Thursday, Friday, Saturday, and Sunday. The last nights to fall into the drinking routine were Monday and Tuesday, and that's how we continued for many years to follow.

In addition to relying on alcohol, I always carried decongestants and painkillers with me. The only way I could function was to take them every four hours, sometimes every three and a half hours. But, as I mentioned before, I was an expert at burying my concerns, and the alcohol and the pills all helped me numb my pain and my thoughts so I could get on with what I had to do.

During my time at Marquette University, I changed majors a few times. I switched out of physics because it was a purely mathematical science, and I wanted a hands-on experience. I fell back on Spanish, which I'd studied in high school until I realized just how poorly prepared for college Spanish I was. Then, I switched to business school. Business school was a natural extension of the family business I grew up with, and I focused on finance because I enjoyed the mathematical side of finance. Numbers came easily to me, and I quite fancied an exciting and high-powered finance job. Fortunately for me, it worked.

I loaded up my electives with accounting credits knowing that I could manage the classes. With hindsight, I know now what a good decision that was. I wanted a sexy finance job, and accounting is far from sexy, but I've since learned that finance majors land sales jobs while accounting majors land accounting and finance jobs. So, I got there more by accident than by design.

There was a problem, though. All the switching of majors while in college had put me behind in credits. Molly was behind in credits, too, so we took classes in the summer when there was hardly anybody on campus. I remember the time being quite stressful and having conflicting thoughts that gave me terrible headaches. *I don't want to be here—I have to be here—I don't need to do this—I have to do this,* and on and on.

In the summer, classes were on an accelerated schedule. Since summer classes were scheduled for six weeks with two to three long sessions per week, instead of 13 weeks of one to two short sessions per class, which was how the regular semesters were structured. Summer classes lasted much longer, three hours instead of an hour and a half. Of course, the solution to the stress of intense summer classes was to skip classes early.

Molly and I often left class early, picked up some wine, and went to the beach. Or we went to Summer Fest, a music festival on the lakefront in Milwaukee that was straight down Wisconsin Avenue to the ease of where we lived. There was a huge main stage and three or four smaller stages with multiple acts playing. As students, we got a discount on tickets. We went early each day, around five o'clock in the afternoon because the shows were not reserved seating, so we could pick our spot. Molly wanted to sit up higher in the bleachers so she could see over the heads of everybody seated at the ground level. We picked spots on the bleachers just high enough up to see the stage clearly and drank wine coolers all night.

At the Moody Blues concert, we sat on the ground level for some reason. We were near the end of the bench in our row. Everybody stood on the benches to see the stage, so we stood on our bench to see also. Then, people started jumping up and down on the benches. This made our end of the bench pop up like a springboard and launch us into the air. We were literally being bounced up into the air in the dark. *I hope I come back down on the bench,* I thought. The smell of pot was so strong a person could get high on the air alone—no need to bring any of your own.

Over the summer, Molly and I went to visit my parents. On one occasion, my dad made an offhand comment, "Why don't you two just get married and get on with your life?"

"Oh, no, Dad," I said, "we're going to graduate first and then get married."

My parents were very supportive of the relationship, but they didn't feel that they had money to spare to help us. They were concerned about how their milk-hauling business was going. Molly's parents weren't supportive at all. They were hoping I'd go away. They wanted Molly to marry some corporate executive's son or the son of a wealthy doctor or lawyer. I came from the wrong side of the tracks and was more akin to something the cat had dragged into them.

Regardless, when the fall of 1985 arrived, we finally said, "Why don't we get married?"

At the time, we were attending Grace Lutheran on Broadway in Milwaukee, which, at the time, was a very neglected church. It needed much love, many repairs, new carpets, and repairs to everything else. Pastor Huebner had just joined. He agreed to marry us despite Molly being Catholic; he only asked that she take Bible education classes for six weeks. Once a week, she'd take a class, and then he married us on November 30, 1985.

Molly's parents tried to discourage her relatives from attending, but her aunts and others made the trip to Milwaukee for the wedding. Her parents refused to attend. In total, we had somewhere between 15–20 guests at our wedding. Molly and I waited at the back of the church until the pastor asked us, "Are you ready?"

We looked at each other, then walked down to the front and had the religious version of a judge marrying us. The vows were barely more than "Do you take her?" and "Do you take him?" with a brief religious message. The ceremony lasted 20 minutes, and just like that, we were married.

* * *

We were students, we were poor, and we were married. But we still had to finish finals, and we still had to graduate. By that time, we both were out of the dorms. I was living in an apartment at 2001 West Michigan Street, so we lived there at first. It was a first-floor apartment in an ancient building with radiator heat. The wind blew through the windows no matter how tightly we closed them. Inside temperatures wouldn't rise above 50 degrees unless we put thin plastic sheeting over the windows and sealed it with a hairdryer. The apartment had a big porcelain sink with plumbing underneath that disappeared into the stone wall. When the sink backed up, the maintenance man who came to fix it poured acid down the drain.

I asked him, "Why would you do that? The pipe is metal. Acid will eat into the metal."

"Oh, no, no. This is how you clear a clog," he said. Then he left.

Sure enough, it wasn't long before the acid ate through the pipe, leaving us with a large puddle of water, acid, and sludge on the floor. I cleaned that up and called again for maintenance. Maintenance didn't seem to be coming, so I bought a roll of wide clear packing tape and wrapped it around the pipe to seal the hole. I used up the entire roll to seal the hole. It was watertight.

We graduated from Marquette University in Milwaukee in December 1985, in the middle of a recession. At the time, Milwaukee was still a manufacturing town. It's now become more financial and service-oriented. We sat next to each other at the graduation ceremony, which was a small, somber affair for the few December graduates that there were. December graduates wear the hat, and that's about it. They sat out in the auditorium along with anyone who attended to support them. When our names were called, we stood up, waved, and sat down. It was very fast and very impersonal.

We celebrated at the Harp & Shamrock, our home away from home, with rum and Coke.

5. THE JOURNEY

had been struggling all along in many ways from my childhood and through college. I was taking large doses of over-the-counter medications and mixing in alcohol to numb myself up and to sleep (poorly at best). It took me a long time to come to grips with the fact that I had serious health issues and needed to seek help. I had to finally face my problems, and stop fighting, resisting, and denying them. Ultimately, help brought me to a better place emotionally, psychologically, and physically.

* * *

My journey with my health began as an ill infant. My parents lacked the money to buy medicine for me at one critical time when I was ill. At that time, one farmer that my father collected milk from gave him 10 dollars as a thank you for some good advice. Ten dollars was a considerable sum in those days, and my father used it to buy the medicine I needed.

I don't remember noticing many differences between myself and the other kids in Kindergarten and first grade, but as I moved on into second to third grade, I suspected something was not quite right. The other kids could all outlast me, run further and faster, and throw harder and farther. I thought if I worked harder and tried harder, I could too. I was wrong.

Try as I might, I was always left wondering, *Why do I tire so quickly? Why am I the one who's the slowest? Why can't I throw the ball as far or hit the ball as hard?*

I always felt tired and needed a lot of sleep. I never woke up feeling rested and had no idea why. Everyone seemed to have more stamina and energy whether we were playing football or watching a movie. I was always the one who couldn't stay awake. I wondered why I always had sinus problems, colds, and bouts of flu. My parents were the same. They were always taking over-the-counter drugs, and as a child, it didn't take long for me to become an expert at picking out the right medicine from the cabinet in the bathroom when I wasn't feeling great—Tylenol, Advil, Tylenol Cold, Alka Seltzer.

Also, as a child, everybody said I snored a lot and very loudly. I wasn't getting a good flow of air when I slept. Physically, I have a small mouth. I've had braces twice, which in those days involved pulling the teeth further back into my mouth to correct my overbite, making my mouth even smaller and even more crowded. I've had all my wisdom teeth removed. I've had four more teeth in front removed to make room to straighten out my teeth because I had such a terrible overbite—as a child, I was terribly self-conscious about it.

I was never really excited about going to the doctor or the dentist. I found it to be a terrifying experience for a long time. As a kid, I was so nervous about seeing doctors and dentists that sometimes I threw up from anxiety about possibly hearing bad news.

When I started seeking help in 2014, the number of doctors in my life multiplied quickly over a span of only two or three years as they started to investigate what was going on with me. Once the doctors started helping, I realized, *they're not all bad. Sometimes doctors can make you feel better.*

I soon saw that all the medical professionals prescribed it through the lens of their specialty. I call it "hammer syndrome." To the person holding a hammer, everything resembles a nail: bam, bam, bam. I went to the therapist, and she said, "You're depressed, you're down, and that's why you've got no energy. We've got to work on that." I went to the nutritionist, and she said, "Your diet's not right. No wonder you don't have energy." Everybody's looking at the same symptoms and seeing them through their own lens. As a patient, I felt that I was in the middle. After I had six or more doctors in my life involved in my medical care, I started to think, *Are they talking about the same thing but saying it differently? Who is right? Is this doctor right? Is that doctor, right? Is it the combination of all of that? What is the correct answer?*

When I had a decision to make, whether in business or for my health, I had to distill the best advice I got from different experts and decide what was right for me. It wasn't so much that I was avoiding doctors before this time as it was that my doctors weren't noticing anything particularly wrong with me. They simply stated the obvious. "Oh, you seem to suffer a lot from infections." No shit, Sherlock!

My first surgery was in first grade for a hernia hydro-seal problem. Today it's an outpatient procedure, and I had to spend three days in the hospital. I remember waking up from the anesthesia feeling as if I had been run over by a freight train. I couldn't believe how groggy I felt. I was strapped down, so I couldn't move around much, but I managed to wriggle around to a more comfortable position.

In those days, visiting hours ended at 8:00 p.m. Everybody had to leave, even parents of young children. One night I was crying because I was alone and sad. Some people, relatives of another patient down the hall, came to see if I was alright and stayed with me for a while until they had to leave. When I finally left the hospital, I had to stay at home for six weeks to recover. Every day the bus stopped, and an older kid ran up to the door with a stack of books and homework and collected the work I'd done from previous days. I couldn't wait to go back to school.

I was good at burying my concerns with my health, and it took until I was married and with children to really do something about it. My family kept saying something was wrong.

"You're snoring really loudly and keeping us awake," they complained.

I knew I wasn't sleeping well, wasn't breathing very well, and generally wasn't feeling well. I was living on alcohol and high doses of over-the-counter medications. I often woke up gagging and gasping with acid reflux. Antacids didn't help. I later learned that your breathing causes gagging and gasping, which then causes acid reflux, not the other way around. When you reach the point where you're gasping for air, the gasping pushes stomach acid up into the esophagus.

The tipping point to seeking medical help came when we took a family trip up to Door County, Wisconsin. We stayed in

Sturgeon Bay where we shared a single room with double queen beds. Door County is in the eastern part of Wisconsin, it is the thumb that sticks up into Lake Michigan. Sturgeon Bay is a city in Door County, not the bottom part of the thumb near Green Bay, but halfway up the thumb. There are beaches, scenic areas, and places to go kayaking. The kayaks have clear bottoms; you can look down to see shipwrecks.

On that trip, everybody in the family complained about the noise I made at night. By the time the trip ended, I stopped denying that I had a problem and decided it was time to seek help.

During the third week of September 2014, I found a clinic on the west side of Chicago in a suburb called Schaumburg. There, the doctor performed sinuplasty, septoplasty, and turbinate reduction surgery to help my breathing. It didn't solve the problem, so I searched for another clinic and found Dr. Michael Friedman, an ear, nose, and throat specialist in the city of Chicago. Dr. Friedman had a sleep center on the north side of Skokie.

Just before Thanksgiving in 2015, just two months after finding him, Dr. Friedman performed "a revision." He redid the sinuplasty, septoplasty, and turbinate reduction surgery, because the first procedures weren't effective. This time, mechanically, the air was flowing, and I was breathing better, but I still wasn't feeling any better. I was still tired constantly.

I underwent three sleep studies with Dr. Friedman to check for sleep apnea. For these sleep studies, the nursing staff placed electrodes all over me and told me to "relax and go to sleep." The first time I did the sleep study, I slept a total of one hour that night. I chose to do each sleep study on a Thursday night, so I could stumble through Friday and go home and relax over the weekend.

Sleep apnea is when you stop breathing for a brief time, whereas sleep hypopnea is when you experience very shallow breathing that is not enough to oxygenate the body. The sleep studies measured these two things. During episodes of sleep apnea or hypopnea, the body is starved for oxygen, and you wake yourself up choking and gasping for air. As a result, you don't sleep well, and, consequently, have no energy. This was happening to me frequently each night.

The doctor diagnosed me as having more than 26 sleep apnea episodes per hour. Approximately every two minutes, in some way, shape, or form, I was waking myself up to breathe. I didn't remember it, I wasn't fully awake, but I was never falling into deep REM sleep. The doctor wanted to fit me with a CPAP device—a mask over the nose and mouth that helps to force air into the body—but I didn't think the device was for me. I said from the beginning that I wanted an oral appliance instead. The oral appliance is a two-piece retainer with upper and lower parts that interact to push the lower jaw forward slightly to open the airway and allow more air to flow on each breath. But first, I had to convince the doctor and the insurance company that a CPAP would not work, and that the oral device was the best solution for me.

I knew if I had to stick something on my face at night, my claustrophobia would keep me awake, and I would not be able to sleep. And sure enough, that is exactly what happened during the sleep studies to set me up with a CPAP device. In fact, for the CPAP sleep study, I didn't sleep at all. The facilitators told me to pack up and go home at three o'clock in the morning, because they weren't collecting any data. After that failed sleep study, I was fitted with an oral sleep appliance. It helped with the sleep, but I still wasn't feeling better.

Next, in June 2016, Dr. Friedman referred me to Dr. Payel Patel, who was the immunologist and allergist in his practice. Dr. Patel ran an extensive battery of blood tests. She found that my body was not producing antibodies. Hallelujah! Finally, an answer! It wasn't the answer I wanted to hear, but at least we were starting to figure out what was going on with me.

Dr. Patel proceeded to use the Pneumovax 23 vaccine, which treats 23 strains of pneumonia. I didn't have pneumonia, but the goal was to see if my body would produce an immune response. The results came back in August, and I had no immune response. She then tried Prevnar 13, which is formulated for 13 strains of pneumonia. The big difference between the two vaccines is that one is protein-based and the other one is not, so there is often an immune response with one or the other.

I had to wait eight weeks after each vaccination to see if my body would produce an immune response. In the middle of November 2016, I received a call from Dr. Patel informing me that there was no response to the vaccinations. She informed me that my condition was chronic, lifelong, would not go away, and that I needed immunoglobulin replacement therapy. Up to that point, I was holding out hope that the doctors could fix me. Now, it was a case of you're *going to have to undergo treatment for the rest of your life, and oh, by the way, it's horribly expensive because the medication relies on people who have the heart to walk into a plasma donation center and donate plasma.*

Three days before I started treatment, I gave up alcohol for good. It was March 26, 2017, the day before my daughter's birthday. I wanted the alcohol out of my system so that the treatments would have maximum effect. I was concerned with what might happen if I abruptly stopped drinking. Would there be any problems? After 24 to 48 hours, I had no withdrawal effects, and I haven't had a drink since.

The immunoglobulin treatments that I undergo are made from donated plasma, and the solution is difficult and costly to process. Donated plasma must be sanitized and checked to make sure it does not contain any viruses that could be passed on, and then the batches of plasma are mixed and broken down into various component pieces of plasma. Currently, the Ig replacement solution I use is one of 24 biological medications that are manufactured from donated blood plasma. Another biologic made for plasma is the medication used to treat hemophilia.

My treatments are once a week, and I administer the medication at home. Usually on a Tuesday evening. Vials of immunoglobulin solution and infusion supplies are delivered to me every four weeks. The immunoglobulin solution looks like water, but is thick and sticky and irritates the skin, if it comes into contact with the skin. Each week, I insert six needles into my belly, tape them down, and hook them up to tubing that flows through a valve that controls the flow rate of the immunoglobulin solution. I connect that valve to large 50ml syringes that I filled with the immunoglobulin solution extracted from the vials. I insert the syringes into a syringe pump, which compresses the syringes and forces the immunoglobulin solution into my subcutaneous tissue so my body can absorb it.

I start each infusion by getting all of the supplies for the weekly infusion out of the supply box. I lay out the sharp little extraction tips, the syringes, the flow-rate control valve, and the infusion needle set which branches out into six needles on a pad. I also lay out the Tegaderm patches, alcohol wipes to sanitize the vials and my abdomen, spot bandages, and a gauze pad. The Tegaderm patches hold the needles in place in my abdomen during my infusion. I check each vial of immunoglobulin solution to see if the solution appears clear like water. Cloudiness in the solution indicates a potential problem. After my infusion is complete, all needles go into my sharps container and the other used infusion supplies are discarded in the trash.

I remove the part of each vial's label that has the serial numbers, batch numbers, tracking numbers, and manufacturing numbers for that batch. I keep these label parts in my infusion logbook for future reference. If it is discovered later that a bad batch of immunoglobulin solution was shipped, I can search back through my logbook to check to see if I received part of that bad batch. I also record the date, infusion start time and stop times, and other health-related details. I pop the protective tops off the vials and sterilize them with alcohol wipes. The sharp tip called an extraction point goes on the big syringe, and I empty the vials into the syringes. Then I attach one of the syringes to the valve and the valve to the needle set. I push the solution through the valve and needle set until it almost reaches the needles to force the air out and to prime the needles.

At that point I started poking the needles into my belly. They need to be spaced two inches apart and two inches away from my belly button. I try not to reuse the same place repeatedly because that causes scar tissue to develop over the years and scar tissue can become so thick that it is difficult to insert the needles. I was surprised to learn just how hard it is to push a skinny little needle that I could barely see into my skin. Skin is much tougher than I ever realized. When I am careful about inserting the needles straight into my skin, it generally doesn't hurt much. When I am inserting the needles at an angle or into a nerve, I know immediately because it is quite painful. I tape each needle down with a Tegaderm patch. After all six needles are inserted and anchored in place, I pull back on the plunger of the syringe to check for blood, which would indicate that I inserted a needle into a blood vessel instead of subcutaneous tissue. If I can draw blood out of one of the needles, I clamp the hose to that needle shut and do not use it. The immunoglobulin solution is meant to be absorbed gradually through my subcutaneous tissue not injected directly into my bloodstream.

Then, I start the syringe pump, which takes 12 and 14 minutes to empty each 50ml syringe.

After the infusions, I tend to feel a little bloated for a couple of days. Between infusions, I pretend that I'm normal and healthy until my next infusion day arrives. Then, I cannot pretend any longer that I am normal—I'm sick, I've got a body that doesn't work, and it sucks!

The cost of the immunoglobulin treatment is approximately $100,000 per year. I also receive injections of Xolair every four weeks to control my autoimmune disease, which costs approximately $50,000 a year. Xolaire controls my autoimmune urticaria and vasculitis. Vasculitis is a skin rash that makes me look like I have a horrible skin disease that could be contagious. There are big reddish streaks up and down my arms or legs—mostly my legs—that fade into a brownish color before completely fading away. While vasculitis is flaring, it looks awful and is not a good look at the gym. Urticaria is itching and burning welts on the skin. It's the strangest sensation, both itching and burning at the same time. I was at the point where I couldn't sleep. I was getting so tired. I was practically walking into walls.

My doctor also prescribes hydroxychloroquine, cetirizine hydrochloride, and famotidine, all of which are over-the-counter drugs to control allergic reactions and heartburn. They're well-known as Plaquenil, Zyrtec, and Pepcid. I take these medications two times each day. The goal is for me to taper off these medicines after six months with no urticaria or vasculitis reactions. There is some concern that has the potential to cause eye damage. Before I started taking it, I had a baseline eye scan so that my eye health can be checked each year. And lastly, I carry EpiPens because there is always the risk of a reaction to my immunoglobulin treatment and a blood clot.

People frequently ask me how I can have both an immune deficiency and an autoimmune disease. It's because one part of my immune system doesn't produce antibodies, so my body is always at a low count. My body is a bit like a car that's always leaking oil. You always have to add oil, that's the immunoglobulin. But the car has another problem; it overheats, that's the autoimmune conditions flaring up and attacking my body. So, the Xolaire suppresses the autoimmune response. I often describe my body as being a quart low and overheating. Together, these conditions cause other problems in my body, allergies, breathing problems, asthma, gastrointestinal problems, muscle and joint pain, sleep problems, and more.

In late February 2019, I saw a gastroenterologist. She discovered I had an irregular heartbeat and referred me to a cardiologist. Leaving that appointment, I expected that it would take some time to set a referral appointment with a cardiologist. Molly and I went to have lunch at a local restaurant, and during lunch, I received a call telling me my referral appointment with the cardiologist was already scheduled for later that same week. *Wow, that was quick,* I thought, *they're not messing around.*

At the cardiology consultation a few days later, the cardiologist did an EKG, and said, "I'm noticing PVCs."

"OK. In English," I said, "What is a PVC?"

I learned that PVC means premature ventricular contractions—part of the heart beats a bit early. And then the question was, "Can you feel it?" I wasn't sure what I was supposed to feel. I didn't feel anything unusual. The cardiologist's concern was that if the PVCs occurred more than 30 percent of the time, they would need to medicate me. I asked, "What types of medication?" The doctor told me they use beta blockers. I said, "What are beta blockers?" The doctor gave me two or three names of what he preferred to use. When I looked them up, I saw that fatigue was right near the top of the list of side effects. I said, "No way! I'm already dragging and can barely function at times. I don't need something that makes me more tired." I sweated over that for a while.

A week after I saw the cardiologist, on a Friday morning, I went to the hospital so they could attach a Holter monitor. I wore that monitor until mid-Saturday morning after I went to my scheduled OrangeTheory Fitness session. The cardiologist told me to follow my normal routine, but to NOT shower while wearing the monitor. The monitor was sweaty when I took it off Saturday morning and put it in the monitor storage bag. I returned the monitor Monday morning at the hospital.

"How come it's all wet?" the nurses asked, because they were concerned they might not be able to read the data on the monitor. I told them I'd worked out and hoped the monitor wasn't too wet to read the data. It wasn't, and the PVCs measured eleven percent. So, I was good; I didn't have to worry about beta blockers. I saw the cardiologist a year later for a follow-up. I had seen my regular primary care doctor shortly before that appointment for a physical, and my primary care doctor had said, "Oh, the whole PVC problem doesn't seem to be an issue anymore." I went to the cardiologist appointment, and the cardiologist said, "I'm getting even better readings than your primary care physician." That, for me, was a huge relief.

My immunologist worried about some blood results she was seeing on my blood tests early on and sent me to a hematologist. Going to hematology is not the most comforting thing to do. Hematology and oncology reps paired together in every hospital I've ever been to. So, I was sitting in a waiting room next to people who were dying from cancer, and I was waiting to see a hematologist because some reading on a blood test looked odd. The hematologist looked at it and said, "It's no big deal. Your readings aren't that strange or abnormal."

Later, my immunologist was concerned again about these same blood test results and sent me back to the hematologist. The hematologist said, "That reading is not going to change. It's going to be that way for the rest of your life. I'm not worried about it." End of story as far as he was concerned.

I have periodically been sent to a rheumatologist to rule out Lupus. The rheumatologist I've seen said four markers need to be present to diagnose someone with Lupus, and I only had one of the four markers. So, no Lupus as far as the rheumatologist was concerned.

As you can imagine, dealing with medical insurance is no party. Approvals and preauthorizations from my insurance company for my immunoglobulin replacement therapy used to come near the end of every year when I had my insurance with Blue Cross Blue Shield. I never felt that Christmas came until I held in my hand my approval and preauthorization to continue infusion treatment during the following year. There were years when it was December 26 or 27, and I was thinking, *where is it? Where is my preauthorization?* I depend on my insurance to keep me healthy and in the land of the living.

Now, with my current insurance provider, Ambetter, as long as I sign up for the same insurance plan year in and year out, my approvals and preauthorizations, which are no longer calendar year based, will typically roll over into the next calendar year. If I change insurance plans in January, I have to go through the approval and preauthorization process again before January to ensure my infusions are covered on my insurance plan. Otherwise, I only go through the approval and preauthorization process when the existing approvals and preauthorizations expire.

I became self-employed in 2020, and I signed up for a plan through Ambetter, one of the two companies in Indiana that sell Affordable Care Act-compliant plans. I'm not actually on an ACA plan, however. Through my broker, I was able to qualify for what is termed an off-marketplace plan. By choosing the premium I was willing to pay, I could adjust my out-of-pocket and some other benefits. Here's a tip, if you're willing to pay a few more dollars in insurance premiums, you can lower your out-of-pocket and layer on some additional benefits.

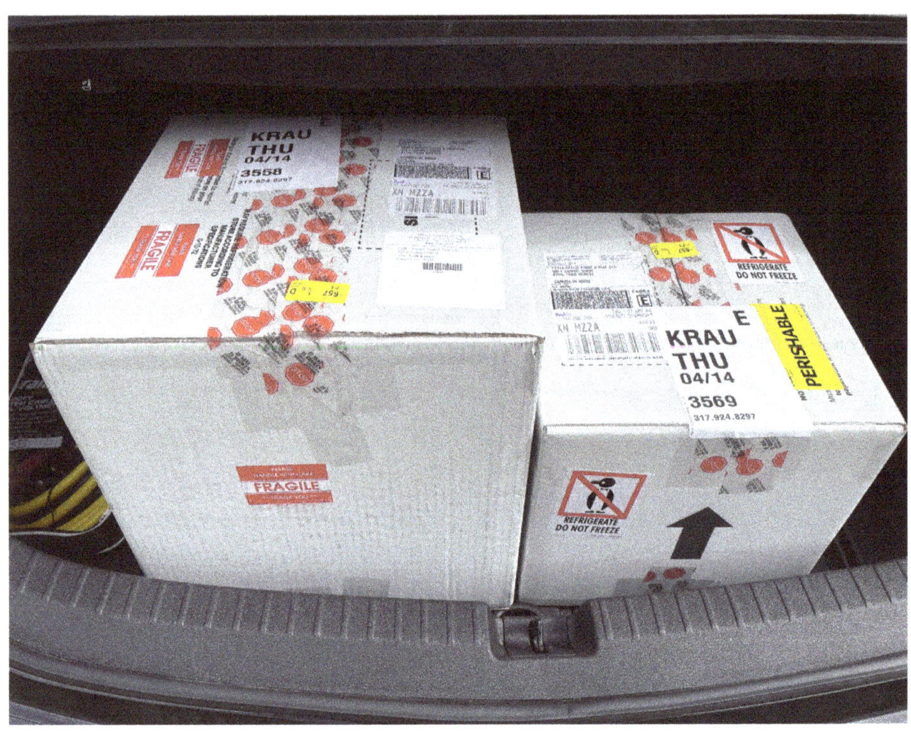

A four-week supply of my immunoglobulin therapy, delivered to my local FedEx office, now in the trunk of my car.

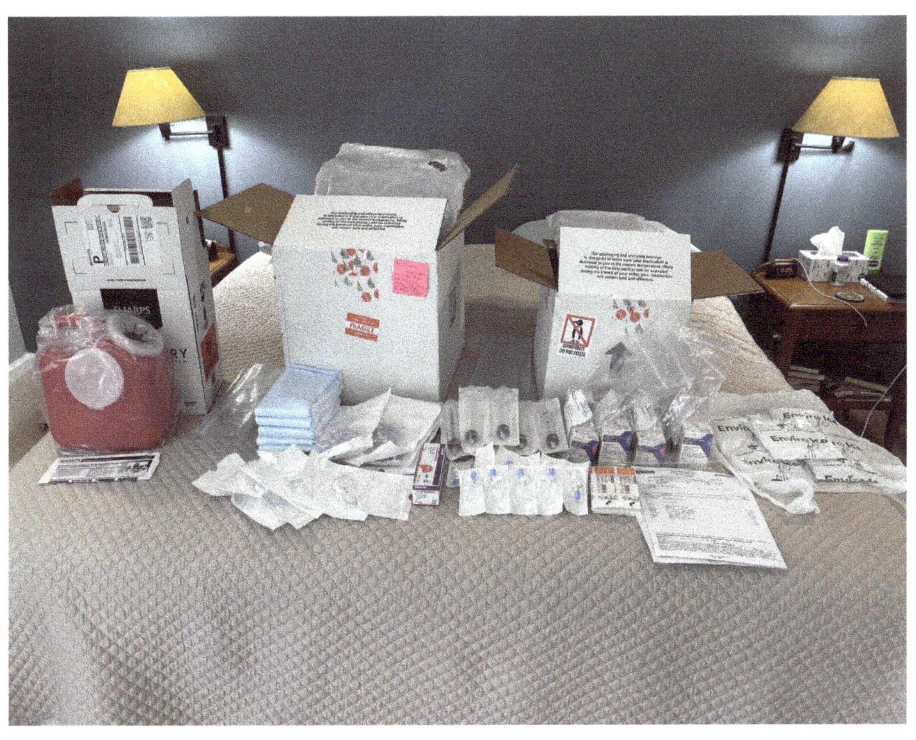

The contents of the boxes for my immunoglobulin therapy. It is delivered every four weeks.

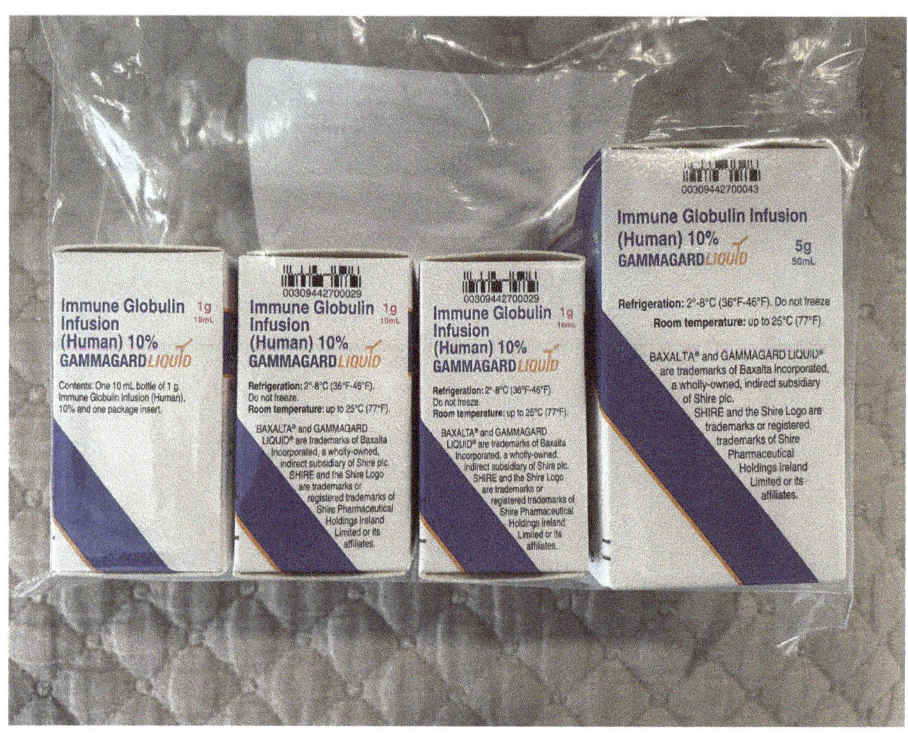

The immunoglobulin solution that is manufactured from donated blood plasma that I infuse each week.

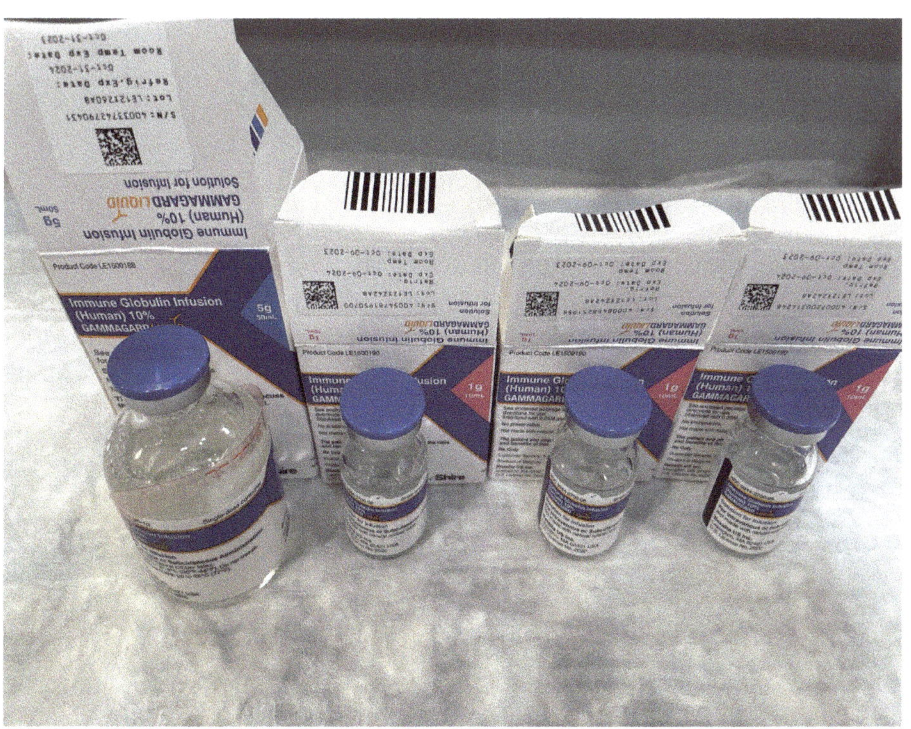

The vials of the immunoglobulin solution that I infuse each week.

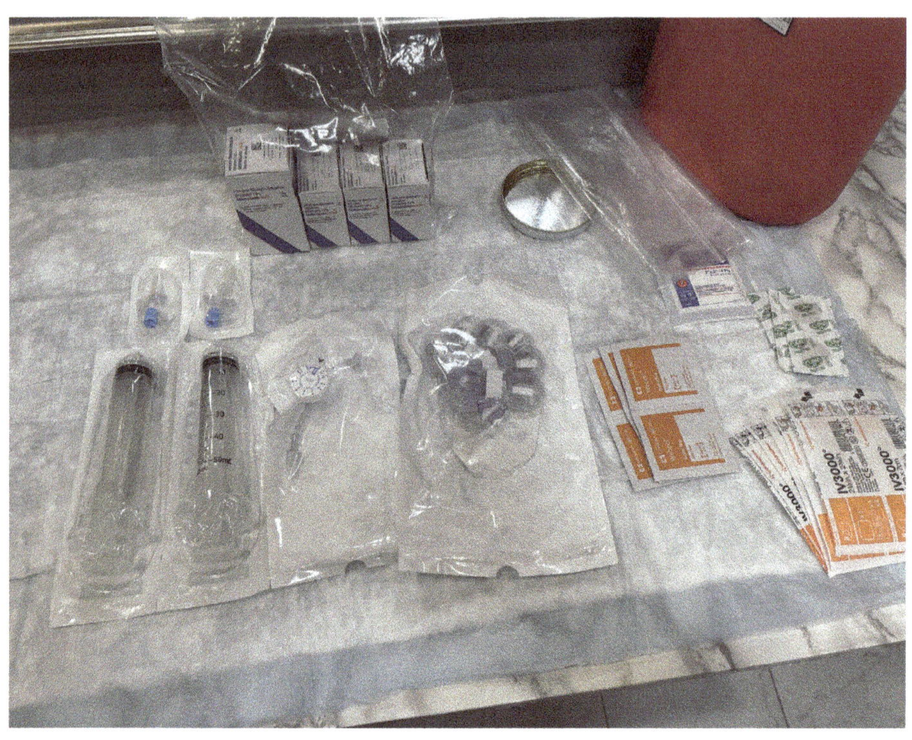

My weekly infusion supplies laid out and organized for my weekly infusion.

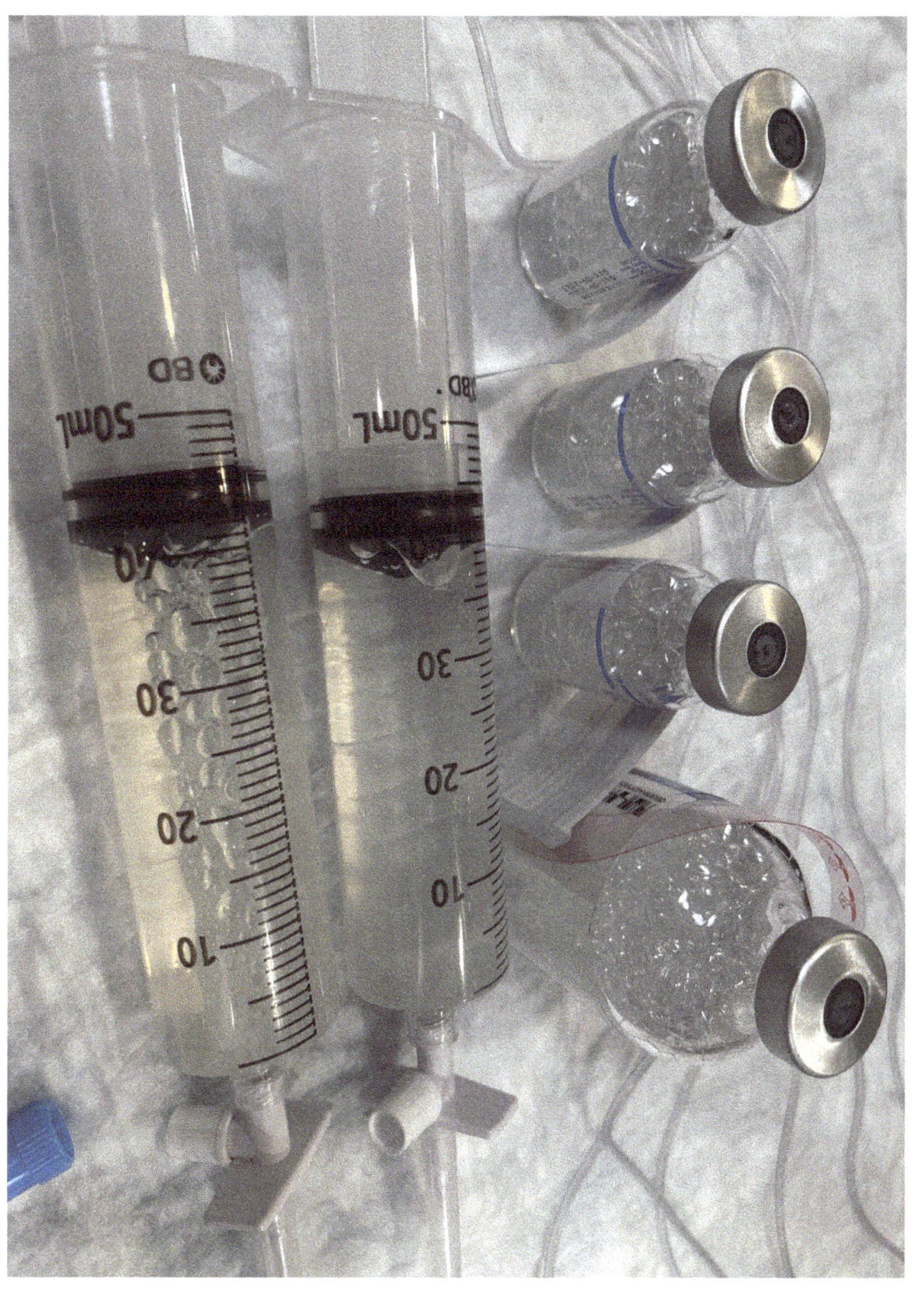

The 50ml syringes loaded with the immunoglobulin solution after it is extracted from the vials.

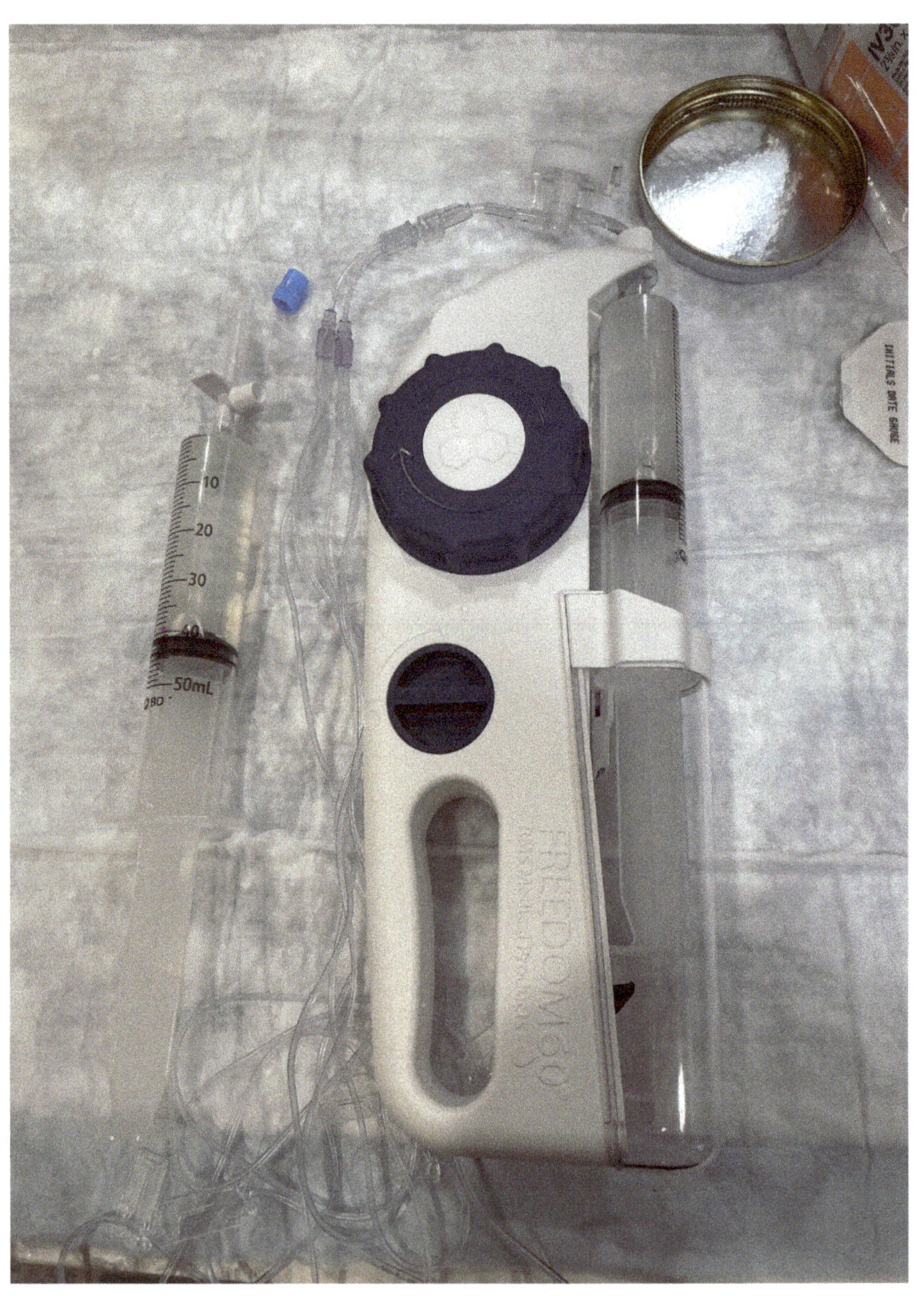

A 50ml syringe in the syringe pump and the tubing with the infusion needles. It is connected to the regulator valve.

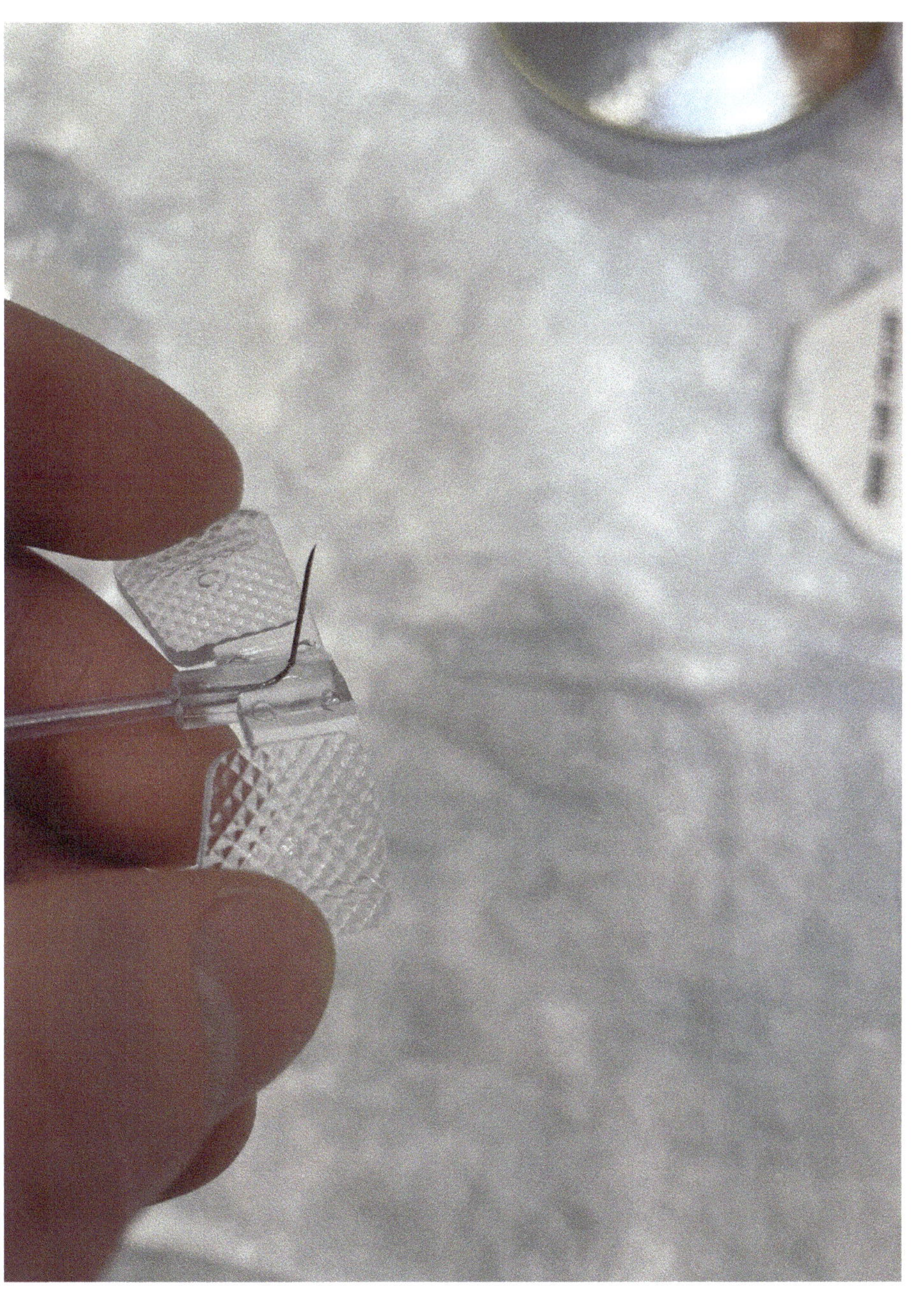

A close-up of one of the six 9mm/27 gauge needles that I insert into my belly for each weekly infusion.

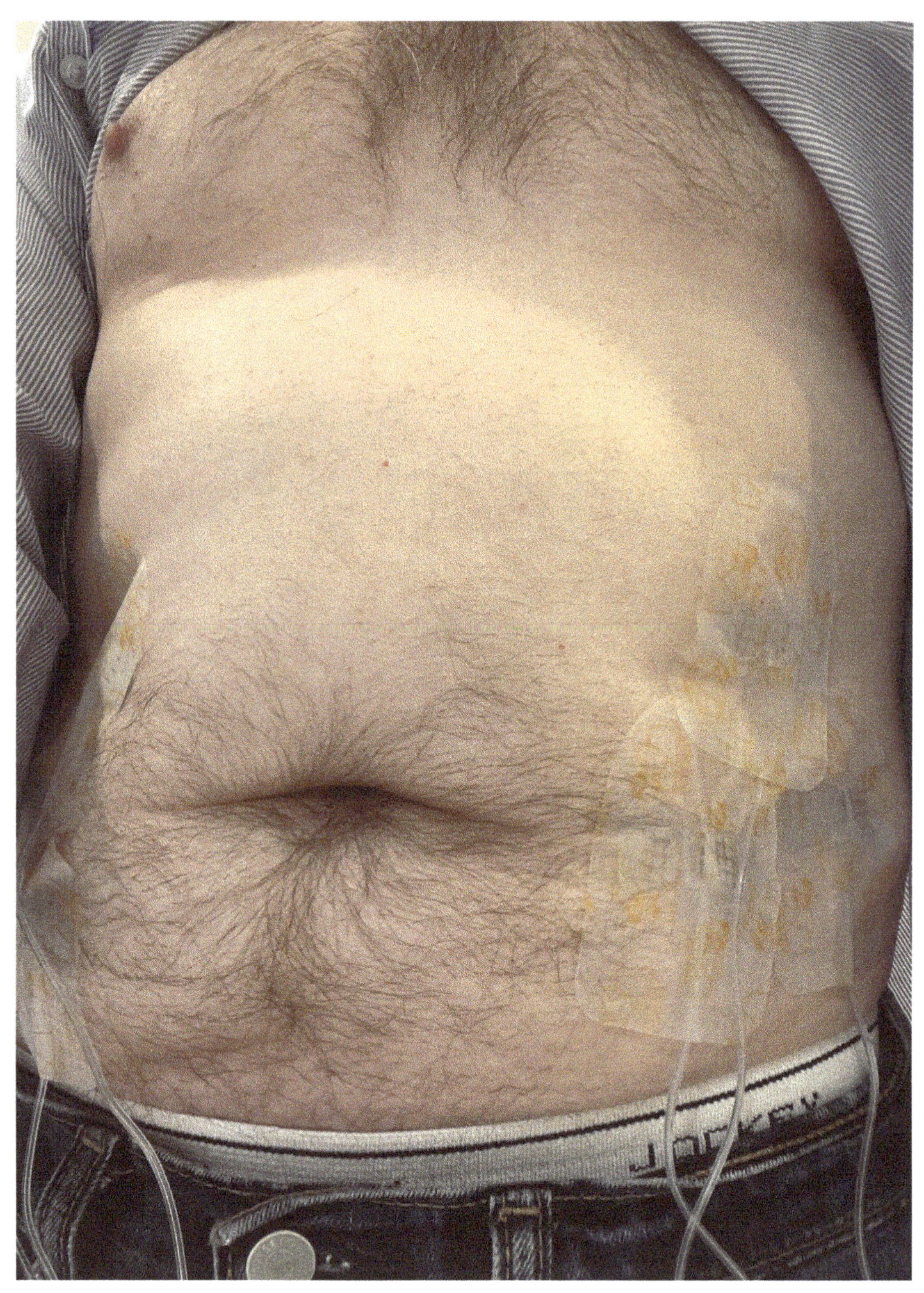

Six needles inserted, held in place with Tegaderm, to infuse the immunoglobulin solution over the next 28 minutes.

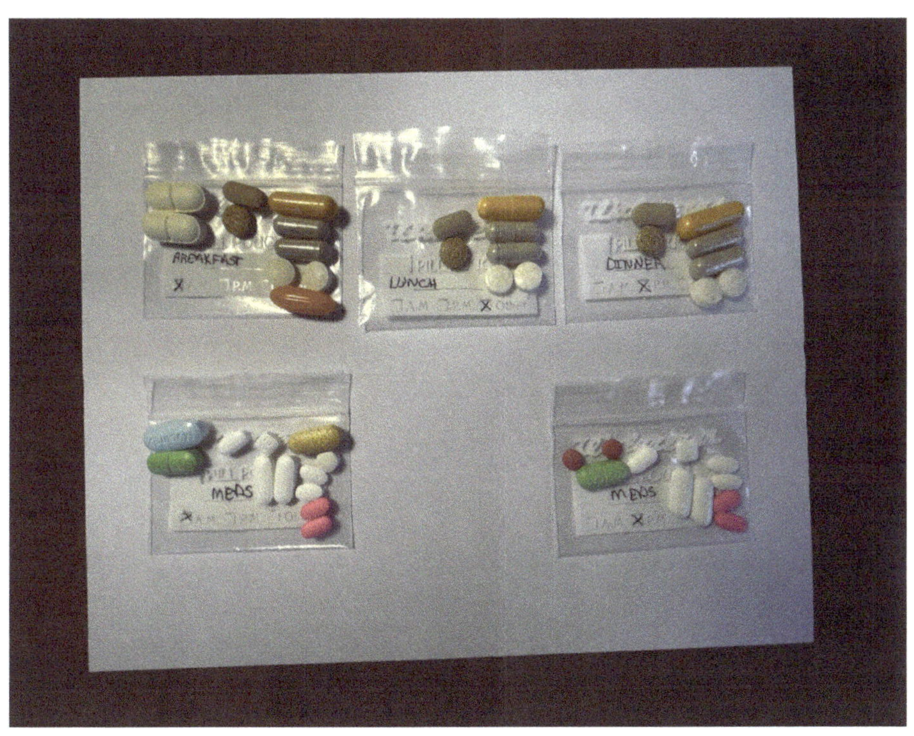

Some of the daily medications that I take to control my various illnesses.

My immunoglobulin therapy supplies ready for each weekly infusion.

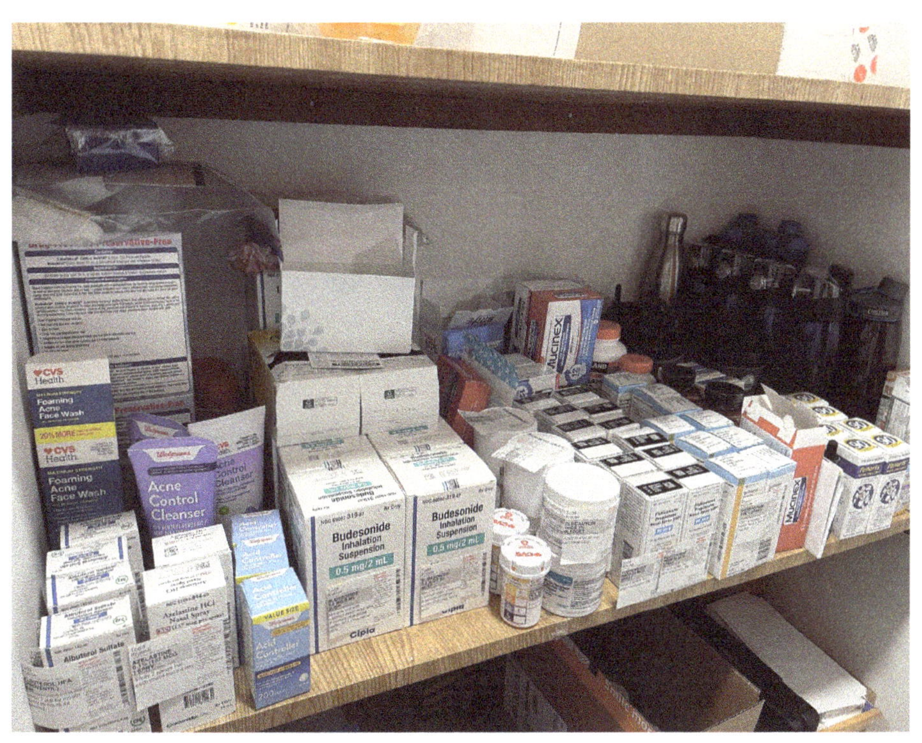

A partial view of the medical supplies and medications that I use on a daily basis.

6. THE WEIRD WORLD OF ASSETS

Now to my career. When I say to people that my career in finance was not at all conventional, they look at my job titles and say, what do you mean? I have two graduate degrees—an MBA with a 4.0 and a master's in accountancy with a 4.0, and I am a CPA. That's not particularly strange, I agree. Also, the world I worked in used standard job titles and organized companies the way any other company in any other industry is organized. I held controller, chief financial officer, and chief operating officer positions, all of which seem pretty conventional. But that's where the comparison ends, because the work I did was unlike the work in any other industry. I'll walk you through it.

* * *

Molly and I had married on November 30, 1985, and graduated from Marquette University in mid-December 1985. Two months later we had our first car payment—$101.20 a month for a Plymouth. The car was unreliable and spent more time in the shop than on the road. It didn't really matter, because with us both earning $3.35 an hour at temporary jobs, we had no money to go anywhere anyway. We stayed home, paid our bills, fed ourselves, and kept the lights on and the place heated.

My first job after graduating was a temporary job for the tax season. I was working for the First Wisconsin Trust Company. I knew nothing about taxes, but my supervisor told me what numbers to find and where to put them on the forms. That much I could do.

At the office, we sat in the old-school style. The first person at the front of the row was the most junior. The person behind that was the first person's supervisor; the person behind them was the second person's supervisor, all the way to the department head at the very back of the row.

I reported to Grace. She suffered from migraines. I could tell when one of her migraines was coming on—things suddenly became quiet behind me, and then I'd hear her rattling around in her desk drawer, looking for the bottle of big fat pills. If it was very bad, she'd call her husband on the phone, saying, "Hello, Tony, can you come get me?" Her husband would pick her up, and her car stayed in the parking garage overnight.

In an effort to find better, full-time work, we moved from Milwaukee to Palatine, Illinois, a northwestern suburb of Chicago with the help of my parents in June 1986. Milwaukee at the time was largely a manufacturing city, and the economy was in a slump, so there was little work to be found that was permanent employment. My parents offered to assist us financially with the move on the condition that one of us had a job in the Chicago area. Molly found a management trainee position with Bill Knapp's restaurant, and we moved to Palatine. I searched furiously for six weeks to find a job and started at William Mercer & Company in August 1986.

I commuted 13 miles east on Lake Cook Road to William Mercer & Company. When I started, it was A.S. Hanson, but they were in the middle of a buyout as I was being hired. Suddenly, six to eight weeks later, the company announced a buy-out by William Mercer & Company.

My salary was $17,400 a year, which wasn't a lot even in those days. My job was certifying pension benefits, what I call paralegal work. We were given big fat books—all paper at the time—containing pension plan documents and a few sheets of paper explaining each retiree's situation. There were notes and binders telling us how to calculate monthly pension payments for the union workers. In some cases, these retirement payments might be $220 a month or less after years working for the company. *These people probably worked 25 or 30 years, and they're only getting a couple of hundred dollars a month,* I thought.

Despite Molly and I both having full-time jobs, we were lucky to have $5 or $10 left for the weekend. Our incomes were so low. We found a bar in Palatine where, on a Saturday night when the right bartender was there, we could buy one pitcher of beer with our $5. And sometimes, if he was feeling generous and happy, he'd give us a second one for free. That was the highlight of our weekend.

We had overwhelming debt. Most finance experts recommend paying off your most expensive debts first, such as high-interest credit cards. We didn't have much spare cash left for a big payment, so I paid off the smallest loan first. That way, we at least had some more spare money each month that we didn't have to use to pay a loan, a few more dollars we could use any way we choose. We didn't follow the conventional advice, but it worked, and we slowly paid down the debt from school and from starting our life together.

From Palatine, we moved to Des Plaines—south and somewhat east. The entire time we lived in Chicago, we seemed to move progressively east, toward the lake. We lived in Des Plaines for two years and didn't go to church much during that time. From Des Plaines, we moved to the west side of Northbrook for about five and a half years and lived in the Salem Walk apartments on Milwaukee Avenue. We didn't go to church much during that time, either.

Then we moved to a townhouse, closer to the center of Northbrook. Our place faced north onto Walters Avenue, which was an east-to-west street. At the end of the block was Shermer Road. Each morning, I ran across Shermer Road through the parking lot to the commuter train station to catch a train that went to the Loop in Chicago. We lived there for almost seven years—two days short of seven years to be exact. We attended a Missouri Synod church called Grace Lutheran that was three or four blocks to the west. Later, when the kids came along, we started going there regularly.

I didn't do well at William Mercer & Company. I didn't enjoy it, so I searched for a new job. When I left, I got a 35 to 40 percent bump in pay just for going down the street to Henry Crown & Company. I worked for a woman manager in the Crown family office; it was a three-billion-dollar-plus family business. The family had about 200 professional people working for them, doing all their bookkeeping, accounting, and taxes.

The first office I worked at was on Washington Street in a building that's no longer there. Next, the company moved to 222 North LaSalle Street, which the Crowns owned, but they had sold the land underneath it to a Dutch firm. I remember sitting at my desk wondering, *How does that work? You own the building, but they own the land. What happens when they say, "You're done—get out?" Do all the employees pick up the building and march it across the street to another piece of land that the company owns?*

The Crown family at one time had owned the Empire State Building. I found that out when I was sent to the top floor where all the records were stored to dig through some boxes for some specific records. *What? The Empire State Building? Are you kidding me?* I got nosy and looked in a couple of books. The books were the accounting records for the Empire State Building from a couple of generations ago. I couldn't believe what I was seeing and what these financial power families actually do. Most people think financial investors focus on mutual funds, stocks, and bonds, but they're missing ninety percent of what actually goes on inside of wealthy families.

I stayed at the company for about three years. I don't know that I got along all that well with my manager. Her group had a high turnover. When I was hired, the company desperately needed somebody and was happy to have me. She had one of those desktop calendar pads where you rip the top sheet off every month. She wrote down what time everybody came in. "Todd came in at 8:15. Jim came in at 8:20." She'd keep score on everybody there just in case she needed to pin something on them. I'd never seen someone so vindictive.

I was happy to leave Crown—it wasn't right for me. I don't feel good about how I left them, but when I got a new job at Harris Associates, I didn't tell Crown that I was leaving. I was the last one in the office on my last day there. It wasn't all that late, only shortly after 5:00 p.m., but the others had already gone. I ripped my nameplate off my cubicle and put my resignation letter in the middle of my manager's desk and slammed my nameplate down on top of my resignation letter. I was angry with how I was treated by her.

* * *

Harris Associates was where life turned around for me. While at Harris, I completed my two master's degrees in night school, took a CPA prep class, and sat for and earned my CPA credentials on my first try, all while working full-time. During this time, Molly called herself an "MBA widow." Then, when I was working on my MSA—Master of Science in Accountancy, she said, "I'm an MSA widow." When I was studying for the CPA exam, she said she was "a CPA widow. "

It's true that it took up a great deal of my time, attending night school for the master's degrees and the CPA test prep and the CPA exam. I remember being utterly exhausted much of the time. It wasn't much easier for Molly, but it was to benefit us all, so we accepted the hardship.

I was initially hired by Harris in the mid-1990s to do the accounting and back office operations for their hedge funds.

When I started, Harris was a $2.5 billion company with around 90 employees. Years before, the partners of Irving Harris had bought the business that became Harris from Irving Harris. At the time when I started working at Harris, the partners who ran the Acorn Funds convinced the mutual fund board to let them spoil the Acorn Funds off from Harris, and Ralph left Harris with the Acorn Funds, worth about a billion dollars at the time, and a dozen employees of the firm.

Everyone thought Harris was on the ropes and dying after the announcement that the Acorn Funds were leaving, but Harris never missed a beat. Harris started the Oak Mark Funds before the Acorn Funds could legally exit. It was an extensive process to move the whole Acorn Fund family that involved many months of planning and work. By the time Ralph marched out the door with the Acorn Funds and his group of employees, the Oak Mark Funds were not only open for business, but twice the size of the Acorn Funds.

My role at this point was taking care of hedge funds. But I was fairly new in the office and still trying to understand the investment strategies. When they weren't busy taking care of client money, the partners invested in private deals. One of those investments was an alarm company in Los Angeles that was going great until, all of a sudden, it wasn't. The partners wanted to know why.

I'd been at the company for about six weeks when they threw me on an airplane headed to Los Angeles to figure out what had happened with the alarm company investment. When Harris initially gave me this assignment, I thought they were nuts. *Are you sure you want me to be the one to check this out?* I thought.

It turned out that the alarm company was thriving at first —buying up little mom-and-pop alarm companies and moving into the largest headquarters of whichever company they bought as they expanded. That worked out fine until the CEO decided he needed his own headquarters, a private limo, and a private jet. His business wasn't large enough to pay for that level of opulence, so that was one of the last investments the alarm company made. The alarm company went bankrupt, and the investors received eighteen cents back for every dollar they invested.

Michael was my direct manager, and he worked for Peter, who was the top producing partner at Harris. Michael told me the following story about Peter and the other partners. Whenever the partners were experiencing an economic drought, they would describe themselves as being in Africa on a safari and a hunt. As the story goes, while all of the partners would sit around the camp moaning and groaning about how bad the hunting was and about how they were not finding any game to shoot, Peter would be out beating the bushes. He would manage to scare up a tiger, and as the tiger was running through the camp, Peter would be running behind shouting to the other partners, "Catch him! Grab him! Shoot him!" The point of the story was that no matter how good or how bad the economy was, when all the other partners were moaning and groaning, Peter always seemed to be able to find new business.

Peter had a huge corner office on the fourth floor of Two North LaSalle Street in Chicago. It was stunning. He had a gigantic table that he used as a desk with a thick slab of marble on top and a worn-out leather chair to which he was devoted. The leather was split, and stuffing was coming out, but he would not give up that chair no matter what. Peter also smoked in the office. He'd keep his office door closed when he smoked his large cigars.

I did investment analyses for Peter. I worked for weeks on these reports to try to make them perfect, and then he'd call me into his office when my reports were ready. I'd start by knocking on the door, "Peter?"

"Yeah, come on in."

The whole office was blue with cigar smoke. I literally parted the clouds with my arms as I entered.

"Peter, are you in here? Oh, there you are."

The haze parted. I could see him in his old leather chair at his huge desk. He had me stand beside his chair as he looked over my report. He loved Ticonderoga number two pencils, and he'd flip through the report as his pencil moved along an inch above the different numbers.

"Uh-huh, uh-huh, uh-huh," he used to nod as he scanned the page. Then, the pencil would stop and hover above a number. "How did you calculate this?" I'd tell him.

"OK," he'd respond as he flipped the page.

"Uh-huh, uh-huh, uh-huh," and then, "How did you calculate this number?" I'd tell him.

He'd flip the page, and then somewhere along about page three or four, the pencil would stop. He'd circle a number and say, "That's wrong."

Oh, God, I'm thinking. *I worked for weeks on this report. How does he know what's wrong in five minutes?*

Well, now I know. When you live and breathe investments daily, you know the relationships between the numbers. And when something doesn't flow in a certain way, you start to sense something's not right. He had all those years of experience. He knew that when one number changed, another number also had to change by some amount. He instinctively knew the relationships between the numbers on the reports and could spot an anomaly in an instant. It was amazing.

The analyses I did for Peter were related to the 22 private deals the partners of Harris owned and to other deals he was evaluating for potential investments. The projects ranged from potential investments in oil and gas to coal to the alarm company to Japanese art, to a bottled water vending company, and more. The partners were invested in water vending years before water came in little plastic bottles bundled together, 12 or 24 in a pack. With the bottled water vending system, you took your empty jug to the machine in your local grocery store, paid the appropriate price, pressed the button, and filled your bottle with filtered water.

If there ever was somebody you'd want to partner with in business, it was the founding partners I worked with at Harris. They didn't let people around them down. Even when the alarm company investment was failing and I reworked the projections in the numbers, we sat in Peter's office and searched for a way to make it work. They didn't give up on things. "What if we do this? Would that work?" I went back and reran the projections with the change, but every avenue we explored ended in failure fairly quickly. My advice to them was to cut their losses and get out. But their response was, "No, we're their partners; we've got to make this work."

I found the trust that I had lost in people was restored to a great extent working at that firm, and it was comforting to see people with strong ethics. Peter had a woman named Fran working for him. Her condo had a fire while we were working there. Peter personally helped Fran and took her cat for medical care. The poor animal was covered with soot and partially burned, but Peter put him on his lap in his big fancy Mercedes and drove him to the vet. He didn't say, "I'll call somebody." He did it himself. I learned a lot from those people.

Besides the alarm company, I saw only one investment that went sour—an oil investment. Their timing was perfect, but in the wrong direction. The company caught it at the top and rode it to the bottom.

As the founding partners were retiring, one by one, the newer, younger partners did not want to continue investing in these side deals. I was asked to liquidate them, and I did. Liquidating most of their investments was easy. But the oil and gas investment was tricky. How do I sell an oil rig so we can close down and liquidate the oil and gas partnership? The industry is heavily regulated; the government has many rules about this type of activity, and the EPA was watching closely too. We couldn't just place an ad in the paper and say, "Oil rig for sale, ready to go!"

I called the person who had originally organized the deal and said, "Help. We want to liquidate. What should I do?"

"Deep breath," he said. "OK, breathe, breathe. We can do this; I'll help you."

Sure enough, he helped me sell the oil rig. In the meantime, I soaked it all in at Harris and began to see what it was I really wanted to do.

* * *

Sometimes, when the schedule lightened up at Harris, the office staff noticed and took advantage of the free time. When that happened, several of my coworkers and I went out for a long lunch. These lunches developed into a sort of ongoing quest. I don't know quite how it started, but Don came back one day and said, "Oh, you've got to check out this Italian restaurant. They've got the best tiramisu."

"OK, that's the restaurant we're going to," we decided. "We'll check out the tiramisu." Then someone came in a few days later and said, "Oh, no, that's not it—I found one that's even better."

We went to that restaurant the next time. It became our "in search of tiramisu" adventure every time we had one of those two-hour lunches during the lull times.

* * *

Harris hired me initially to specifically oversee the operations of the one existing hedge fund. That one fund grew to five hedge funds managing over $500 million in investor assets. I worked in the alternative investment side of Harris from 1990 to 1996 when I transferred to the corporate side of Harris where I worked until I left the firm at the end of March 2001.

Initially, I managed the entire accounting and operations for the hedge funds by myself by working long, crazy hours. Slowly, over time, I figured out how to organize my work better. The better organized I was, the less time things took. For example, I found that if I was holding a piece of paper—and I know from experience that the auditors want a copy of it, and so do the tax people—then before filing it, I made copies for the auditor and the tax staff and dropped the copies into folders for them. Then I wouldn't have to dig in the file room for it again at the end of the year for that piece of paper. But the real lessons I learned were about how the company invested and why these investments worked.

I advanced to Controller at Harris over the 11 years that I was there. Molly's parents finally started to accept me, although I thought it unfortunate that my value to them only increased as I earned more money and more exclusive job titles.

As the original founding partners I'd known and learned from moved on or retired from Harris, I began to think it was time for a change. In 2001, I left Harris Associates to join Anchor Asset Management. Anchor was a very small company with a European clientele. They were a U.S.-based asset manager with offshore funds based in the Cayman Islands. Shortly after I started there, there was talk of spinning out the back office and creating a separate company. I wasn't sure how I felt about that because I had just started working there, and now they were talking about carving me and the back office operations out to create a separate company. But forge ahead with that idea we did, and it served me well shortly afterward.

But then September 11, 2001, occurred, and the whole world changed. The event shook everybody's confidence. All the European investors panicked and wanted their money back. Everything stopped. And I mean everything: money movements, wire transfers, clearing checks. Everything stopped globally for about three days. We had international clients on the phone, saying, "I want my money, I want my money." The clients were scared.

We told them, "We can't give it to you because the world's financial system is not moving. You can have your money back as soon as the world's financial system opens up and starts moving again." That was really the beginning of the end for Anchor Asset Management. It didn't survive that trauma. The partners called the staff into the office and laid off everybody except me. Then, they asked me, "Can you shut the company down in six weeks?"

"No way. Six months minimum," I told them. "You've got accounts all over the globe. You have legal structures that need audits, tax returns, and much more. For an orderly liquidation. Six months is the minimum."

"OK, fine," they said. "Get going."

In December of 2002, things were more or less in order for the shutdown. The partners called me into the office and said, "OK. We'll take it from here." With that, I was released from my position.

Anchor Asset Management fell apart at that point and soon went out of business.

Meanwhile, over a period of months, I had been working on setting up my own fund administration company. I even found a partner with help from the company we office with.

I describe what my partner and I did at that time as building an airplane in the air with no safety net. On December 30, 2002, I was let go by Anchor Management and had both feet in a fund administration company that we called Trident Financial Services, LLC.

This was not a good time to be looking for a job, so my partner and I had to make it work one way or another. I started calling everybody I knew. Little by little, Trident Financial Services was winning business. We could pay ourselves and our bills. Honestly, 2003 was scary, but everything in my life up to that point had prepared me for this. I'd had so many near misses I wasn't afraid of risk. I was used to hard work, used to having meager resources, and I had a dogged determination that made me take one step at a time and break the insurmountable down into manageable bites.

But then things took a turn. My partner didn't know the fund administration business, and he didn't know the industry. I brought in a person to help with marketing, but the Trident itself needed stabilization. In late 2003, I added my marketing person as a partner. As we found my original partner was not up to the task of helping to operate a fund administration company, we bought him out. Then in early 2004, I hired a person to help with operations. I wanted him to focus on operations and human resources to stabilize that part of

Trident so I could focus on the work we were delivering to our clients. I was also involved in the sales process, not so much with generating the leads, but with helping close the leads and onboarding the new clients.

That year, 2004, surprised us all. It was magical. Trident grew and grew. We kept every client. We didn't lose a single staff member—an amazing record of zero client turnover and zero staff turnover. Along the way, my partner, who was my former marketing person, and my operations person put their heads together and decided that they would push me out of the company.

My partner, who was my former marketing person, confronted me on a cold, dreary, windy afternoon in April 2006. He had booked a private room at what was then The Sears Tower. I presumed that privacy was required so that he could yell and scream at me while he shoved me out of Trident. As it happened, though, his reservation for the room wasn't secured. My guardian angel had struck again! Hallelujah! We sat at the bar instead, where he had to be civil while telling me he could run the company better than I could.

The problem was that the shift toward technology in our industry was in full motion. Clients expected web portals, electronic statements, and the ability to sign in and see their accounts. We had none of that. We used Excel, we used Word, and we were smart people, but we just couldn't compete. We couldn't keep up no matter how fast and how hard we ran.

This confrontation happened in mid-April 2006. The next couple of months at the office were quite uncomfortable for me, and I imagine they were for everyone else too. I was trying to figure out what to do, and my partner was making things very miserable for me. I focused my energy on finding the next opportunity. After I left Trident, my partner hung on and kept Trident going for another 12–14 months before Trident all collapsed, because it couldn't effectively compete. As the business started to collapse, my partner fired my operations person, and my operations person was back out in the street.

While I was searching for my next opportunity, I heard from Paul at ABN AMRO LaSalle Bank. The bank division he was in had permission to start a fund administration unit. Paul had a business development background. At LaSalle Bank, Paul was part of a three-person team tasked with creating this new fund administration unit. Their problem was they didn't know how fund administration worked. They needed someone with this expertise. Paul found me through LinkedIn, and we met for a conversation over coffee.

"You're the one we need," he told me. "You know how fund administration works. You know what the accounting and taxes look like and what the day-to-day operations involve." As a result of that conversation, I became the fourth member of the startup team for that business unit at LaSalle Bank. I had the title of First Vice President—I was three layers down from the CEO on the organization chart, and those top layers at large banks are really thick. I couldn't believe that, somehow, I'd landed among the top 50 people at the bank. I only realized this when I was later invited to an executive company dinner.

The executive company dinner was a super plush event, held at the LaSalle Street building, an elegant old building that the bank owned. The top of the building has a beautiful and ornate dining facility with marble, linens, and elegant wood finishes. We attended in full suits and ties. As I waited there in the hallway for the doors to the dining room to open along with the other members of the bank who were invited, another person told me, "Oh yeah, this is the top 50 people in the bank."

I remember thinking, I don't feel I'm a top 50 person. I feel like that duck who's swimming calmly on top of the water but whose legs are paddling furiously beneath the water.

Earlier, during the third week of June 2006, I started at LaSalle Bank. I was hired by the head of the CDO business unit. LaSalle Bank had been acting as a trustee for structured products called collateralized debt obligations (CDOs) and collateralized loan obligations (CLOs). These were the products that later brought down our financial system in 2008 and 2009.

The market was booming along in 2006, and it had really picked up steam around 2004 and peaked in 2006. The deal sizes kept getting larger. Originally, the deal sizes were around $150 million. By the time I got involved, the deal sixes were in the billions of dollars. The largest deal I ever worked on was $3 billion. Everything just imploded in 2008.

The money managers in the structured products market wanted to go out to the public market to raise more money so they could keep growing and keep creating CDOs and CLOs. A requirement for entering the public market and asking for investor money is to produce the GAAP-based financial statements, which are required by the SEC. Lasalle Bank had a trustee reporting system, not a GAAP-based reporting system.

The bank had no one who knew how to produce these GAAP-based reports for CDOs and CLOs. I had the necessary expertise and quickly learned the finer details about CDOs and CLOs, which I researched in depth after I joined LaSalle Bank. However, I still had some lingering questions I was unsure about. I went to the senior people at the bank and told them I needed the answers to put the final pieces in place necessary to produce GAAP-based reporting. They arranged through high-level contacts a meeting with PricewaterhouseCoopers for my accounting manager and me in New York. She and I boarded an airplane early in the morning to New York to meet with the experts at 300 Madison Street.

Security at the PriceWaterhouseCoopers building issued us picture IDs with a security barcode. Everything was so efficient and sophisticated in their New York office. We took the elevator up to the correct floor. The doors opened, and we entered an exterior hallway that only looked out over the city. We couldn't see any of the interior of the PricewaterhouseCooper's operations. We were shown to a conference room that, again, faced outward.

Eight of the PriceWaterhouse people sat on the side of the conference table opposite my accounting manager and me. Some were tax experts and some financial. A woman sat at the far end with a laptop and recorded every word that was said in the room. I quickly realized that they were afraid of liability, that something they said might be misapplied or incorrect, and it would somehow come back to haunt them. They allotted four hours for the meeting. There were snacks on the credenza, and within approximately two hours I had the answers to all of my tax and financial reporting questions.

At that point, my accounting manager suggested we take an earlier plane home. So, that's what we did. We went back to LaGuardia Airport and rebooked ourselves on an earlier flight.

The GAAP-based accounting was critical to growing the fund administration from $0 to $14 billion quickly. I participated in the meetings and acted as the closer to the line reassuring the clients in such a way that they were confident that we knew what we were doing, which made them eager to sign up. For example, I'd tell them, "This is what you need. This is why you need it. This is how we're going to do it for you. This is exactly what we will deliver to you. These are the people who will do it. These are the people you talk to. If you have questions or you feel like you need more, here's the chain of command," and so on. By the time I'd finished, they were signing on the dotted line. When I had worked at Anchor, I had asked one of the partners how to attract and win new clients. He said, "It's not that hard. You just tell people who you are and what you do." So, that is exactly what I did.

I had started at the bank in mid-June 2006, but there were soon rumors about changes afoot, and the bank was in play. We knew internally but couldn't talk to anybody about it. We couldn't say anything, because, at that time, a potential buyout was not yet public knowledge. The staff received the official internal announcement of the buyout in January 2007, and the public announcement went out in February 2007 followed by an immediate lawsuit from the consortium that lost the bidding war for ABN AMRO LaSalle Bank. In April 2007, the Dutch courts announced that the buyout could proceed. There were two consortiums bidding for the ABN AMRO LaSalle Bank combination. Three giant banks— Barclays, Santander, and Bank of America—won the rights to buy out ABN AMRO LaSalle Bank and split it up along geographical lines.

When large companies, especially large banks, have a significant change in ownership, they schedule numerous days they call Day One's. There's Day One for the new name, Day One for the system changes, and Day One for customer and client account changes—they're all on different days, as everything switches over to new processes and systems. The old company eventually fades away out of existence. Meanwhile, I was coming close to Day One of my new life.

All of a sudden, my world ground to a complete halt. Bank of America is a retail bank, so they were not interested in structured products and funds administration business units they acquired when they bought LaSalle Bank. They viewed our division and all of the business units in our division as a liability. Bank of America began selling off the business units that they did not want to own. That put me back in the job market.

It turned out to be an excellent time to leave the structured product world. Structured products were exactly what brought our financial world to a grinding halt in 2008 when they imploded—the CDOs and CLOs that brought down our financial system in 2008 were what tripped up our financial system for close to a decade afterward. But I had safely moved on, and escaped unscathed, yet again.

I moved on to Ziegler Investment Management and became the CFO for the investment unit. My title was Senior Vice President and Chief Financial Officer. I had two titles—one for their mutual funds because I signed all the financial reports, and another title inside the company structure.

Ziegler Investments had a family of mutual funds called the North Track Funds. In addition, they had brokerage operations and managed individual separate accounts. My responsibility as senior vice president and chief financial officer was primarily for the mutual funds. I had about 10 direct reports. The North Track Funds were a small family of mutual funds worth about $1.2 billion on a good day. There was a plethora of paperwork for the funds, because the reporting was required by the SEC for mutual funds. The paperwork was complex, voluminous, and mind-numbing.

Ziegler hired a woman named Raheela to expand and improve their marketing efforts. Raheela started around the same time as I did. She was having great difficulty making anything happen, and as the days and months went by, it was an enormous source of frustration. I too was having problems getting anything done. My understanding when they hired me was that they wanted me to help them grow the funds. I looked closely into the operations of the funds and came to the same conclusions that all my predecessors had. Everything

I tried to do was stymied. Finally, I went to the CEO who had hired me and asked him what was going on. There was a long pause. Uh oh. I thought. Here it comes. Zieler had a mutual fund board of directors from heavy hitters, such as Fidelity and Vanguard. These directors thought a mutual fund family adding up to a billion dollars was a joke. They thought a mutual fund family should not have a single fund that had less than a billion dollars in size.

It turned out that management had been ordered to sell the mutual funds in a meeting with the mutual fund directors on the Friday before I started. So, when I walked through the door Monday morning to start my job there, it was no longer about fixing problems and growing the funds, it was about keeping the lights on until they could sell the funds. It wasn't long after that they let the marketing director go, and I figured it would be my turn soon. I was told again and again, "Don't worry. There's a seat on the bus for you." But I looked around at the company and thought, Where does somebody with my skill set fit once you sell the mutual funds?

I furiously searched for my next job opportunity and found one with Zacks Investment Management. I actually received the call during a mutual fund board meeting confirming that I got the position. The embarrassing thing about it is I had forgotten to silence my phone. So, my phone went off a couple of times during the board meeting, and I scrambled to push the button on the side to silence it as everyone in the room stared at me. I could feel my face flush with the heat of embarrassment.

I was hired as chief operations officer at Zach's and was responsible for individual accounts, brokerage operations, and their family of hedge funds. I started on January 12th, 2009, and was fired a year and eleven months later on December 15th, 2010, right after Molly and I celebrated our 25th wedding anniversary. What a downer right after the high of such a milestone in my life.

Zacks was an odd place to work—one of those places where you almost had to pay for your oxygen—the company wouldn't pay for anything. Paying the bills was a monthly battle. I told them, "You signed up for Bloomberg services, you have to pay Bloomberg or they're not going to give you the data."

After being fired from Zacks, I was out of work for a stretch of time. I searched for a new position from mid-December until mid-March. Finally, I found a position at the Adler School of Professional Psychology, purely by networking with people I knew and people I met. Adler wanted me to start at the beginning of April. I took my son on a camping and fishing trip during the last week of March in southern Illinois. The weather never did warm up as predicted, but we caught so many fish that we brought home most of the food we packed, because we had all of these fish to eat.

The stress of losing my job, and other things, was causing an existential crisis for me. Things had been topsy-turvy in the investment world, so I wondered if a job in higher education might be a better option.

From the outside looking in, it seemed a fair assumption. I looked forward to starting at Adler as the controller, but once I got into education, I found out they were not adequately staffed. The school had five-year budgets that showed grand plans for rapid growth and expansion. "We're going to grow, grow, grow, and grow," the school projected.

Everybody wants it to happen that way, but that was not their reality. It was a constant battle of changing projections all the time. We were being asked to change and adjust and manipulate the numbers constantly. It was at the point where the numbers were just funny; they weren't real anymore.

My next job was with NAV Consulting, run by a man named Nav. Most of the people who worked in that firm were from the Rajasthan state in India, a part of India that is often called the Golden Triangle. I stayed there for almost four and a half years.

After NAV Consulting, in 2016, I returned to work for the person who hired me at LaSalle Bank at a new business. He had left LaSalle Bank and formed Courtland Capital Markets. What a fantastic opportunity, I thought. When I got inside the firm, though, it wasn't.

He and I had various conversations over lunch. He wanted me to join the new firm he created after he left LaSalle Bank and help improve operations. When I started at Cortland, I found out that the company was just churning out as much work as possible for clients, and they would promise clients anything and everything, even though they weren't always capable of producing what they promised.

It wasn't terribly long after I started when we were all called into a town hall meeting. There, it was announced that Alter Domus, a Luxembourg-based fund administration company, would be acquiring Cortland. There was some initial euphoria among the Courtland staff, who thought the culture inside Cortland would change. Cortland was grinding through people at an alarming rate. People would be excited to join Cortland, but within a matter of months they were looking ragged and tired and were already searching for their next job. Many of them were gone within nine months. It was not uncommon for people to routinely work until eight, nine, or ten o'clock every night, and there was so much pressure from management "to get it done." Meanwhile, the tools the staff had weren't quite up to the task, so much of the work required intensive amounts of manual intervention, and checking and rechecking until a person could no longer see straight. It wasn't long after the acquisition that the person who hired me at LaSalle Bank became Global CEO, and at that point, it was clear that Cortland's culture was not going to change.

From August 2016 until the end of 2016, I worked solo. Beginning in early 2017, I joined the Strategy and Execution Group after it was created in early 2017. I worked with Andy and Michelle, who were well-versed in fund administration operations and very detail oriented. Still, we couldn't get anything done. At the beginning of 2018, after Michelle left, Andy and I were read the riot act by the person who hired me at LaSalle Bank for not accomplishing more. We had no direct authority to make anything happen beyond working with people and making suggestions. We needed management's help and support to get the staff in their departments to buy into the recommendations and changes we put forth.

I could see the situation ending badly, so when an opportunity to transfer to Carmel, Indiana, and head up a credit team popped up in mid-2018, I jumped at it. This opportunity took me away from Illinois and out of the Strategy and Execution group, which was collapsing.

Moving to Indiana solved some financial problems for us, because Illinois was incredibly expensive with high taxes. During the last couple of years we lived in Illinois, we lived modestly, but still needed to tap into savings just to support our daily lifestyle. We had four adult-sized people and six pets living in a 1,200-square-foot house with three tiny bedrooms and one tiny bathroom. Beyond being eager to leave Illinois, though, I needed to get away from the legacy of the Strategy & Execution group. I needed a fresh start somewhere else.

We resettled in Carmel, Indiana, in August 2018. By the fall of 2019, I could see it was the same; the work situation hadn't improved. On Friday morning, March 6th, 2020, I was fired by Alter Domus.

This was just in time for COVID.

7. ADOPTING

My career in finance had taken an unconventional path because of my involvement with unusual asset classes, and I found it difficult to believe that I rose to the level I did in finance. But my personal life also took unexpected twists and turns. Twenty years earlier, in the early 2000s, Molly and I adopted two children from Korea.

I had been resigned to us remaining a childless couple because we hadn't been able to have children naturally. Molly brought up adoption in the early 1990s when we were in our early thirties. At that time, the adoption agencies had a 1950s mentality whereby the father is the breadwinner, the mother stays home, and the family unit lives in a cute house with a white picket fence with a dog and a cat. That's the environment into which the agencies wanted to see a child adopted. We didn't live that way.

We rented. We both worked. We didn't fit the mold that the agencies wanted. Then, around 1995, Molly spotted an article in the Chicago Tribune. It talked about how the adoption world was waking up to the fact that people don't live as they did in Leave It to Beaver. Some live in apartments. Some live in townhouses. Some live in lofts. Some live on ranches and farms. People had different lifestyles, yet they were still good parents. Molly ripped out the article and held on to it. We kicked the idea around for a while. I'll be honest; I was scared by the thought of adopting. I wasn't sure how I felt about the responsibilities of parenthood.

I had struggled up to this point in life. There were many days when I wondered if I was even capable of taking care of and supporting myself, and now Molly was asking me to assume the huge responsibility of supporting and taking care of children, too. I worried about how we could afford to bring up a child at that point in our lives. The whole idea seemed overwhelming to me, and what if something were to happen to me?

Also, from my perspective, I felt that I was the one who typically had to figure out how to make everything work, especially financially, and how to solve all the big problems in our life—jobs, houses, house maintenance, cars, etc.

In the end, we did move forward, and in 2000, decided to look into adoption. We visited several agencies around town and started learning about the process of adoption at informational sessions. Adoptions in the United States at that point were open adoptions, where the birth mom chooses the family. The agencies all said that every family out there has a match with some birth mom. To us, it felt like a popularity contest.

I was interested in going abroad for adoption, specifically to China or Korea.

"There's no way in hell I'm getting on an airplane and flying to Asia," Molly said.

I kept pushing, saying, "At least let's check it out." International adoptions were a very bureaucratic, paper-pushing process, but as long as you met the qualifications at that time, you would receive a child. Outside the United States, there is great demand for people willing to adopt children. We ultimately decided to go to Korea to adopt. Korea has an extensive and effective foster care program, whereas in China, orphanages raise the children who need adoption.

The Korean process was quick when we adopted our children. The entire process in the early 2000s took us nine months each time, about the length of a pregnancy. Now, the requirements to adopt from Korea are far more restrictive, the age ranges for parents adopting from Korea are lower, and the process is much lengthier. We last heard it was taking two years or more to complete an adoption from Korea, and that information is already eight or more years out of date.

We had three adoption agencies and multiple governmental agencies involved in our life as we completed these adoptions. There was the local adoption agency that did our home study —The Cradle in Evanston, Illinois. The Cradle did not have a direct connection to Korea, so we went to AIAA for our direct connection to Korea—Americans for International Aid and Adoption in a suburb of Detroit. Then AIAA connected us with Social Welfare Services in Seoul, Korea. The Illinois State government was involved, the U.S. federal government was involved, and the Korean national government was involved, as there was paperwork, forms, and processes required by each of these governments to complete the international adoptions of our children.

The only thing we didn't have to pay for was fingerprinting and background checks, which we were required to do multiple times. Since our governments do not communicate with each other, both the federal and state governmental agencies required fingerprinting and full background checks—the same fingerprinting and background checks were performed multiple times, all at taxpayer expense, to satisfy these agencies. I found it ludicrous to think how our governmental agencies all looked at the same information, but required the taxpayers, all of us, to pay for it multiple times. How stupid is that? That's the way our government works.

We were immunized for travel to Korea and required to prove that we didn't have HIV/AIDS in order to complete these adoptions. Overall, each time, the adoption process took us nine months to complete. I kept returning to the thought of how ironic this was, because normal pregnancy lasts approximately nine months.

Throughout this process, we completed mountains of paperwork, collected supporting documentation, and waited anxiously for the child referrals. Each child referral arrived with a few pictures, a few pages of information about the child, and less than a page of information about the child's father and mother. In both cases, the parents of our children were young, not married, and not in a good place economically to parent a child. As raising their children was not feasible for them, they placed their child for adoption. We accepted each child referral. Then, we waited for clearance to travel.

"It's going to be a while, relax," the adoption agency told us.

It wasn't long, though, until we got Form I-171H in the mail. Within a day or so after it showed up in our mailbox, the adoption agency called to say it was time to travel. Form I-

171H informs you everything's complete. But somehow, we received the form in our mailbox before the adoption agency knew about it.

We flew United Airlines to Korea in March 2001. U.S.-owned airlines were not allowed to enter communist airspace, so we flew over Canada and crossed Alaska and the Bering Straits, but couldn't fly into Russian airspace. We flew just outside it over international waters. That took us over Japan.

Some of the roughest air turbulence I have ever experienced was in that 747 over Japan. I have never been on a plane that's gone up and down in the air that much for an hour and a half. Everybody got very quiet. We were all hanging onto our seats until it was over. Once we were past Japan, the turbulence settled down again. Then, we made a quick turn and flew into Seoul to land. We left home Sunday morning bright and early and got there on Monday night. By flying over the international dateline, we lost a day on the calendar as we flew.

We had to spend three days in-country. We were there on Tuesday, Wednesday, and Thursday, leaving Friday morning. We had a chance to do some sightseeing, but not much. That wasn't the reason we were there, of course. The Korean peninsula is about the size of Minnesota. Approximately 80 million people live on that Peninsula, versus six million in Minnesota. Two-thirds of the landmass is North Korea, and one-third is South Korea, but the population is flipped: two-thirds live in South Korea and one-third in North Korea. Approximately half of South Koreans live in and around metropolitan Seoul. The city proper had a population in excess of 13.5 million living in the city itself. Greater metropolitan Seoul had a population more in the range of 20 to 23 million people. It is a vast, gargantuan city.

We think we're technologically advanced in the United States, but the South Koreans were way ahead of us. A panel on each nightstand in our hotel room controlled everything—you could turn on or off any light or any appliance in the room from the panel on the nightstand.

We were there the first week of March 2001 to pick up our son when he was five-and-a-half months old. He was born on September 18th, 2000. Korea in March 2001 was colder than Chicago. We were there during the yellow winds. It's a condition that occurs in early spring when winds start blowing east and south across the Gobi Desert. The winds pick up all this fine silty, yellowish dust and blow it across Beijing and the Korean peninsula. It was strange—as we looked down at the street, it seemed foggy. Then, we looked straight up at the sky, and it was crystal clear with blue skies and sunshine. Everything had a fine layer of yellowish powder on it. Many people wore face masks to protect them from the yellow dust they didn't want to breathe.

We hiked up to the top of Namsan Mountain to the observation tower. My wife thought she didn't need gloves, a hat, or a scarf. As we started hiking, she asked, "Are you using your scarf? Can I use that?" We hiked a little further, and she said, "Are you using your gloves? Can I use them?" We went a little further. "Can I use your hat?"

"Why didn't you bring your own?" I asked, curtly. "I planned for this."

We got to the top and went into the observation tower. The heat turned up so high that it was sweltering in there—we went from the bitter cold outside into a sauna inside. But the view was quite good despite the dust. The yellow winds made everything hazy and foggy, so we couldn't take clear pictures of the surrounding areas of Seoul.

Seoul is this mass of tall, 30 to 40-story apartment buildings. The landscape is rugged throughout the city. Locals described the rugged hills as mountains, but they're not very tall. They pop up throughout Seoul to heights of 3,000 or 4,000 feet. As we traveled through the city, we drove through a valley filled with masses of buildings, then through a mountain pass into the next valley that opened up into more masses of buildings, always, everywhere we went row upon row of 30 to 40-story buildings.

We visited our son and his foster family for the first time on Tuesday and learned that Korean apartments are tiny by our standards. The building that my son's foster family lived in was not particularly elegant. Their apartment was very basic and small. It had one little room, and a living room area, and attached to it was a small kitchen with a tiny table and four chairs. Four people lived there full-time—the baby's foster parents with two daughters and the two children they were fostering at the same time. The apartment had one bedroom and a little bathroom. There was a small balcony off the living room area filled with kimchi pots that we could see through the hazy windows.

Picking my son up the next day at the adoption agency to take him back to the hotel was a bit of an adventure. We'd received a printed paper map of the city to help us find our way to the adoption agency. Looking at the map, I realized that everything was written in both English and in Korean, except for one thing, the name of the adoption agency, which was Social Welfare Services Inc. That name was abbreviated as SWS on the map.

Molly and I left the hotel and got in a cab. We didn't know Seoul at all, so we had no idea which direction the cab was supposed to go. I happened to look out the window and noticed that up on the hill there was a Swiss Grand Hotel. I commented to Molly about that.

"Oh, look, Molly, there's a Swiss Grand Hotel," at which point the cab wound its way up the hill and pulled up to the entrance of the Swiss Grand Hotel. The doorman opened the door for us. We were confused and puzzled.

"No, this isn't right," I said. "We're supposed to be at Social Welfare Services Inc., not at the front entrance of the Swiss Grand Hotel."

We had a big discussion with the doorman who was functional in English. The driver was not. Then the doorman had a lengthy discussion with the driver about the mistake. We were on the wrong side of town, and it was around 4:00 p.m. We were expected at the adoption agency in about 20 minutes, but the agency was at least an hour to an hour and a half's drive across town. The doorman helped us to call ahead and explained that we were on our way, that there had been a miscommunication, and we might be a little late.

The driver wasn't at all happy, but off we went on a white-knuckle drive to the other side of Seoul. We arrived at the adoption agency in record time. During our cab ride, Molly was panicking that the agency would close for the day, and we wouldn't be able to pick up our son. I kept saying, "Well, they're not going to stuff him into a basket, put a blue bow on it, and set him out on the front step with I note that says. Good luck!"

When we arrived, we met the social worker, the foster mother, and our son. The rest of the agency, as far as I could tell, was empty. There was a teary scene where the foster mother and social worker were crying.

It was bittersweet. We realized in that moment that we were ripping a child away from their culture, their heritage, their history, their language, and taking them off to a foreign land where everything is completely different. We were happy to become parents, but at the same time, it was very emotional.

On our ride back to the hotel, the roads were congested with rush-hour traffic. Seoul is congested all the time, but like any large city: worse at the beginning and end of each day. Molly held our son in her lap as we drove back across town to our hotel. As we sat in traffic waiting for traffic lights to change, she took his little hand and waved at truck drivers near us. They honked their horns and waved back.

We were told by the adoption agencies to not be surprised if our son became quiet and didn't really say or do anything or make much noise for up to a month. The explanation was that his neural pathways were reprogramming in his brain as he adjusted from what he experienced and heard and felt in his native culture in Korea to the new sights, sounds, smells, and different-sounding languages in the United States. As his new neural pathways formed, he became more vocal and engaged more with the world around him in the United States.

Adoption experts will always say the first and best choice is for a child to stay with their natural birth parents in a healthy family environment. The second best choice is for a child to stay in their culture with a healthy adoptive family. Finding adoptive parents, leaving their culture, and traveling to a different country is at best a third choice.

Korean society has come a very, very long way in the last 20-plus years since we adopted. Back then, Korea as a society did not have a place for children born out of wedlock or for mixed-race children. Their society was similar to that of the United States in the 1950s. It was still a shameful thing for children to be born out of wedlock. Then, there is another cultural element exacerbating the situation, which is that there are no birth certificates. Instead, there are family registries, and children born out of wedlock become invisible. You aren't given a birth certificate in Korea, you receive a listing of the family in the order in which the family members arrived through history, and then you have your place inside of that registry.

In the cases of both of my children, each of their names was at the very top of an empty family registry in Korean society at that time. They didn't belong to any family. Korean society did not culturally have a way to fit these children in. So, they would have been ostracized in Korea. Korean culture, and the Koreans themselves, are very racially pure. Koreans can trace their bloodlines back 5,000 years. When we, Americans, went over there to help in the Korean Civil War, we created a huge problem by creating interracial children that didn't fit inside the Korean culture. Not only were they born out of wedlock, but they were also mixed race too. That was the primary reason that Korea opened up for international adoption years ago. Since that time, Korean society has become much more accepting of adoption, and the number of children available for adoption by families living outside of Korea has declined drastically as a result.

＊

To travel home, we were given a 9x11 Manila envelope jammed full of documents that the flap of the envelope barely closed. The top left corner was cut off, the envelope was labeled with our son's name, and his documents were jammed inside. The envelope was sealed with tape that said only immigration could open it. A huge staple was rammed through his passport to staple it to the documents. We took that big cumbersome thing and couldn't open it—immigration would be upset if it looked tampered with.

How is it possible to board an airplane, fly to a foreign country, pick up a small child, and fly home with them? I wondered.

When we first got on the plane in Korea, the agents did look at our son's passport. Next, we had a layover in Narita, Japan. When I pulled out the big packet to give to the Japanese security people, they waved us past; they didn't even want to look at it. And guess what the expiration date was on his passport? It expired upon arrival in the United States. He was definitely on a one-way trip.

We were stuck in the waiting area in Japan. It was still considered international space, because we hadn't officially entered Japan yet. As U.S. citizens, Molly and I did not need a visa to enter Japan. As a Korean citizen, my son did need a visa to enter Japan. Since he did not have a visa to enter Japan, none of us entered Japan. While we waited, I thought I would help by taking our son to the men's room to change him. I got there when the cleaner had just hosed down the men's room. Everything was dripping with water. The sinks mounted on the wall had no counters between them. The toilets were also mounted on the wall. There were no flat surfaces to lay him down on to change him except the wet floor.

I returned to where Molly was sitting and said, "In the men's room, things are all wet. There's no place to lay him down that's dry. Would you please change him?"

She went to the women's room, and when she returned, she said, "You wouldn't believe it. They've got a changing room with changing beds. And it's fully stocked with diapers, wipes, and everything you could possibly need."

I guess men didn't change diapers in Japan.

* * *

We found caring for our son at 40,000 feet in an airplane bouncing up and down to be quite challenging. It began as we settled down in our seats. When our son squawked a little bit, the person sitting behind us flagged down the flight attendant and asked, "How long is this flight?" Oh, buddy, I thought. You have no idea what you're in for. This is a 15–16-hour flight. And we haven't even left the ground yet.

He moved to a different row.

As it turned out, we had a row of seats to ourselves, so we lifted the armrests, laid our son down in the middle seats, and crisscrossed the seatbelts in a big X over the top of him to strap him in. We did have to pick him up during takeoffs, landings, and turbulence, but otherwise, we kept him in his seat bed, and he slept most of the way home.

* * *

We kept part of our son's given name. He was originally Chung Kei Woon, which we are told translates as friendly or live happily. Chung was the family name, which in Korea and China, comes first. The generational name comes second, and the individual name is third, completely inverted from the order we use.

It says a lot about different priorities in Korean culture. The family and the group are more important than the individual. The Koreans have a custom of reusing generational names in which all the boys of each generation in a family share the same generational name and all of the girls of each generation in a family share a different generational name, but everyone will have their own unique individual name, which is their personal name. The Koreans customarily reuse generational names over and over in a family.

We saw that pattern with our Korean neighbors, and we'd learned a bit about the culture ahead of time, of course. We dropped "Chung" because that was a family name and kept Kei Woon (as it was Americanized), which was incredibly confusing to everybody.

His middle name is Erik with a K, which was the name we picked out. I noticed later that Kei Woon's good friends, the people who care, make an effort to learn to pronounce his name correctly. But currently, he's using the nickname Sky.

Kei Woon is really into cars. Before we left Chicago, he bought a 1970 Buick Skylark—blue with a black top. His nickname, Sky, comes from the name of his car. It's been his baby. It's now on its third engine. This time he changed it from a 350 to a 455 big block. When Kei Woon rebuilt his car, he'd go through automotive catalogs, calculating everything: "I need this part, this part, that part, and I need these connectors." He figured out the engine compartment and how everything was going to fit and connect. He ordered everything, and, to my amazement, it all fit and worked.

His current job is as the parts manager at the local Hyundai dealership. He's not the person who helps you when you walk in the door looking to have your car serviced. He sources the parts needed to repair the carts brought into the dealerships for repair and service.

He has the right personality for it. He can go to an event all by himself, and he frequently does, and he comes home with three new friends. How do you do that? I think. He's very empathetic, has a huge heart, and wants to help everybody.

* * *

My son came home the first week of March 2001, when he was five and a half months old. When we were able, we began the adoption process for my daughter. Ka Hee Nicole Krause came home the first week of September 2002, when she was five months old. Our children are almost exactly 18 months apart in age. Again, the whole process of adoption from starting the paperwork to picking our daughter up was right around nine months.

When we chose our daughter's name, we used part of her given Korean and added our family name along with a middle name we chose for her. The adoption process for our daughter was much the same as for my son, but now we knew how to speed through the paperwork. We flew Korean Air and took a different flight path than we had for our son. We took off from Chicago and flew up over Canada and Alaska and across the Bering Strait. This time, though, we flew over the eastern side of Russia. We flew over land for most of the entire trip. There's a big sea between Russia and China in the east of those countries, and ever so briefly, we flew over that. When we got to the Korean peninsula, the plane looped around and lined up for the airport. Between the time we picked up our son and the time we went to pick up our daughter, the Korean international airport had moved from Seoul to Incheon.

We had to take a cab from Incheon to Seoul. It wasn't far from Incheon to Seoul, but it was still a $70 cab ride. The Won to U.S. Dollar exchange rate hovered around 1,250 Won to the U.S. Dollar each time we traveled. We exchanged a couple of hundred dollars at the bank for local currency. The bank teller got out a massive stack of money and put it through a bill counter three times to be satisfied he'd counted it correctly before he handed the stack of Korean Won to us.

We received a huge wad of cash, nearly three inches thick. What the heck do we do with all this? Is this going to fit in a pocket? We both thought. I turned to Molly and said, "You take half; I'll take half." Half was still a thick stack. The hotel cost 1,995,000 Won, between $1,500 and $2,000, when we adopted my son, and it cost us a similar amount when we adopted my daughter. We expected these amounts the second time around. Seoul is an expensive city where prices are similar to those in Chicago, Illinois.

What we'd read about Seoul and Korea in the summer was accurate—you can smell all these aromas as you walk down the street; the kimchi, the soy sauce, and the garlic. The Korean Peninsula is incredibly sticky, muggy, and hot in summer. It is surrounded by water, and it is not a large land mass. The air feels thick and humid, and it's sweltering. With our daughter, we didn't make the same mistake we did with our son. With our son, we kept our regular schedule and did whatever we usually would do. And when he didn't sleep at night, we didn't sleep. We quickly became exhausted. But with our daughter, we'd learned, "OK, she's quiet; I'm going to rest for a while."

Ka Hee did not readily accept Molly as her mother at first. She'd sit on my lap fine, but she did not want anything to do with Molly at the start and barely let my wife hold her.

When we flew back to the United States with our daughter, she howled for about seven hours. I am sure every Korean lady on the plane was coming up to us, offering to help hold her and calm my daughter. We said, "Thank you, but, unless you're coming home with us, we have to figure this out for ourselves."

I ended up literally holding my daughter on my lap for the entire flight back home.

After Ka Hee had been home for a while, there came a Saturday when Molly went out to run errands. I did things in the kitchen, watched the kids specifically, and Ka Hee was playing on the blanket that I had on the carpeting just outside the kitchen doorway. Ka Hee became a little fussy, but I didn't connect it in my mind to anything in particular, such as hunger. But then Molly came home, and, at that point, Ka Hee was just looking for somebody to feed her. Molly grabbed her and got her a bottle and that was the beginning of a real bonding experience between the two of them.

8. EPIPHANY

Now that I had children in my home, it felt essential for me to sort out the financial side of things. When I was out of work starting in March 2020, my instincts kicked in. I did what I typically did when I was looking for a job, which is to cast a wide net. I didn't just look for a corporate job, I also looked for a business to buy and something to invest in.

I spotted an opportunity less than two weeks after my job with Alter Domus ended. A local business in Fishers, Indiana, called The Cleaning Authority caught my eye. Fishers is a nearby suburb of Carmel, Indiana. I immediately inquired about the business, and a couple of weeks later, I started doing the due diligence with the owner. This was a franchise opportunity, and I fancied being my own boss and taking on a relatively simple business operation. I went into the office of The Cleaning Authority franchise to meet and talk with the owner, Bill. While I was there, I also coincidentally met Mirian and had a conversation with her when she wandered into the front office to file some paperwork. Mirian was from Venezuela. She and her family were in the United States seeking asylum because of the dire conditions in her home country. I was impressed by Mirian, the business, and its staff, who were all enthusiastic and seemingly hardworking.

Additionally, I was invested in another investment vehicle—real estate. I wanted enough money to live comfortably and securely. To do that, I had to determine how much money was required each month. I figured out what my monthly budget was, for example $4,000, $5,000, or $10,000 a month, and then I started to create a portfolio of income-producing real estate investments. I didn't really care as much about what the properties were worth as I cared what their monthly cash flow was.

I had always been attracted to real estate. With rental properties, you can start counting doors. Let's say I bought properties and each door pays me $750 or $1,000 a month. If I know my budget, I know how many doors I need to give me enough income. Perhaps it's five doors or ten.

The first property feels that it's an enormous outlay in investment. But with the second, you have income from the first property, so it doesn't feel as unmanageable. Then, when you fast-forward from eight to ten and beyond, the income from the previous properties causes the process to accelerate.

As I write this in 2022, I'm closing on the fourth property I've bought this year in Kansas City; this will be property number 20 overall. I have 13 properties in Kansas City, Missouri, five properties in Indianapolis, Indiana, and two properties in Charlotte, North Carolina.

When I started with the first couple of properties, vacancies drastically reduced the cash flow. I own one property, but it's vacant. That's a 100 percent vacancy rate. With the second one, I thought, It's much better. Now my vacancy rate is 50 percent. Once I got up to numbers eight, nine, and ten, the concern diminished significantly. Now, my vacancy rate on 20 properties is 5 percent with one vacancy.

The property manager I work with in Kansas City is much more responsive than the property manager I have in Indianapolis. The Kansas City property manager helps me acquire properties. I told the property manager what my goals were. I said, "I'd like to have 50 doors and then reevaluate what, if anything, comes next."

We identified three properties in fairly rapid-fire succession and used most of the spare cash I had sitting available to me.

Cash or some form of capital is necessary to invest in anything, not just real estate. I had some help along the way and more recently from an aunt who died on July 9th, 2021. That was nine days before my wife, Molly, died. When my aunt died, her estate was settled, and my late uncle's estate which was held in trust for my aunt were both settled and distributed to all of the beneficiaries. I received some money from the trusts of both my aunt and uncle. Then when my wife, Molly, died on July 18th, 2021, I received her life insurance money, which enabled me to pay off part of the loans I have on my business and purchase more properties. Perhaps, yet again, a guardian angel was looking out for me.

9. LOSS

Molly and I had a non-traditional journey together. My career in the financial world took me to a level I never imagined; we adopted our two children from abroad, and my wife found her own path. Although it came to an abrupt end, I think it worked out the way she had planned. Molly's mother died on March 18th, 1997, of cancer. Perhaps that experience affected Molly and influenced the path she chose. Molly had a stubborn nature. Once she had made up her mind, that was it.

* * *

Molly's parents both smoked and drank heavily, and I'm sure that was the foundation of Molly's heavy smoking and drinking habits, too. Even after we adopted our son and daughter, and Molly had parental responsibilities, she didn't change her lifestyle. She drank a bottle of wine a day and smoked a pack or more of cigarettes a day for years. She would get up, start the coffeemaker, and then go outside for her first cigarette of the day. At least she went outside to smoke.

Molly and I had a good marriage in the beginning, but as time went on, we argued and fought more and more. What married couples don't? Her health declined, and she just wasn't the same person. I had married an inquisitive, energetic person who later in life didn't want to work and didn't want anybody expressing concern about her habits. We typically had a big blow-out fight about once a month. You could say our marriage was stormy. Both my son and daughter witnessed our fights, and at times, were dragged into them.

Molly and I had many conversations about her health before she collapsed in the house on a Thursday night, July 15th, 2021, right around five o'clock. During the last conversation when I had asked her again to cut back on the alcohol and cigarettes, Molly said, "I like smoking." That was one month before she collapsed. I knew a day was coming when we would have to call for an ambulance.

Starting in Illinois, she had developed a hacking, gagging cough that got progressively worse and more frequent, but she refused to go to a doctor. She had a long list of excuses.

"Oh, the food had too much pepper in it. It was too spicy. I swallowed wrong."

"Well, yes, that happens at times," I said, "but not all the time with everything. Something is not right here."

And then, for a while, her excuse was, "I have allergies."

"You know, medicine's pretty good these days at managing allergies," I said. "Let's go find out what's bothering you and see if you can be treated."

But she wouldn't go. I could tell when the kids gave up trying to convince their mother to take care of herself—they stopped asking her to go to a doctor and switched to doing their best to ignore her coughing fits. Anytime friends came over to the house, I could hear the kids at the door coaching them, saying, "Mom's got this gagging, coughing thing she does. Ignore it, and pretend it doesn't happen." Each time

Molly was coughing and gagging, I remember thinking to myself, OK. A day is coming when we will have to call an ambulance.

I remember times when Molly, my son, and daughter, and their friends were sitting around the table when Molly launched into one of these gagging and coughing fits. Everyone continued what they were doing as if nothing was happening. Molly's condition got to the point where she had to run to the bathroom and throw up. This even happened in the middle of the night or when she was sitting quietly on the sofa watching TV. She'd jump up and race to the bathroom because the gagging and coughing made her vomit. Always, she refused to seek help.

About three months before she died, there was a noticeable deterioration in her, physically. She stopped looking like somebody in her fifties and started to resemble somebody in their eighties—she was hunched over and shrunken. I kept thinking maybe the problem was in the throat, maybe her soft palate. Molly's mother had soft palate cancer, so I kept thinking, Mouth, or throat, what is it?

I wasn't really thinking about her lungs, although it had occurred to me that, being a heavy smoker, lung cancer was very likely. I'd already gone through a grieving process for many months before this time, because I knew I'd lost the person I married. She wasn't the same person anymore.

On Thursday, July 15th, I was driving home when my phone started to blow up. My son and daughter were calling me to tell me that Mom had collapsed in the bathroom on the first floor, and they couldn't reach her. Our first-floor powder room wasn't very large, and if anyone was lying on the floor, they would physically block the door. I thought, so today is that day. Now we'll do what we have to do.

I wove my way down our street through all the emergency vehicles until I found a place to park. In my neighborhood, there's not just one or two vehicles that respond, the whole department shows up. When I got to the house, the police sergeant came out and said, "It's your house; you have every right to go in, but they're working on her on the kitchen floor. The first responders need all the room they can get to work on her."

I didn't go in. I had one kid crying on each shoulder. All the neighbors were standing in their yards or driveways gawking at everything going on at the crazy house, our house. You have no idea how much it hurts to have everyone staring at you when your life is falling apart until it happens to you. Nobody, not one neighbor, came over to offer any assistance. We were the freak show, and everyone tuned in to watch.

The paramedics estimated that Molly had gone without a pulse and without breathing for more than seven minutes. The paramedic told me, "If she recovers from this, she will not be the same person you remember." We followed the ambulance to Carmel St. Vincent Hospital. The people in the emergency room said the same thing. "If she recovers, she's not going to be the same person you remember."

When we arrived on the third floor after Molly was admitted to the ICU, the nursing staff there again said Molly would be changed irrevocably if she ever regained consciousness. By the third time I heard that, I started asking, "Is there a person left in that body, or is it just machines and medicine keeping a body alive?" That was Thursday evening. All day Friday, she was hooked up to three medication stands —with four medical pumps on each stand. Each stand held a ring of IV bags with tubes connecting to the pumps and then from the pumps to Molly, forcing medications into her.

Her physical condition did improve some, but she was never able to breathe on her own. Over the next day or so, the doctors removed a few of the medications from her regimen, but the machines were necessary to keep her body functioning. Molly's brother, Patrick, drove all night from Destin, Florida, and he arrived very early Friday morning. Initially, Kei Woon did not want to see his mother in that condition. Patrick told Kei Woon, "I think if you don't at least go see your mom, you're going to regret it for the rest of your life." With that, Patrick was able to convince Kei Woon to go to the hospital to visit his mother.

Saturday afternoon, I was standing in the room—the ICU rooms are positively tiny, and with all those medication stands and machines, there was no place to sit. Each of these little rooms is ringed around a central nursing station so the nurses can closely monitor each patient.

As I stood there taking it all in and trying to make sense of what was happening, Molly's doctor called me to inform me that she was brain dead. He told me we could disconnect life support that same day, if we wanted. He said his recommendation was to wait until the following day so he could recheck Molly's condition a second time. He did not expect his diagnosis to change and told me so.

Patrick, Kei Woon, and I went back to the hospital later on Saturday, July 17th, 2021. The three of us went over in the late afternoon, between 3:00 p.m. and 4:00 p.m. Kei Woon felt ready to see Molly again. Earlier, he went alone with Patrick. This time, the three of us went back to the hospital. At 10:00 a.m. Sunday, we got the call. The orders had been put in to have all the specialists check-in. There was no change in Molly's condition, as expected. My daughter and her boyfriend, Carson, and I took care of everything else.

We said, "OK, let's try donating her organs and tissues."

Carson, Ka Hee, and I went to the hospital around lunchtime. I completed and signed all the paperwork to donate her organs and tissues. We left the hospital thanking the donation process was started and in motion. Not much more than an hour and a half later, I received a call from the hospital saying Molly was not viable as a donor. Scans detected a huge mass in her lungs, which they believed to be cancerous. Now we had a working explanation for what happened to Molly. Her doctors believed that the mass in her lungs grew to the point where it caused her heart to stop beating, and she stopped breathing. It took so long to extricate her from the bathroom that in the meantime, with no heartbeat, no blood flow, and no oxygen to the brain, significant parts of her brain died.

Part of the reason the doctor didn't know what had happened until then was that I had said to them, "I am not against tests and procedures, but would you please answer one question before you run a test or do a procedure: What benefit are we hoping for by performing it? Why are we doing it if you can't answer that question?" The doctor did relatively little testing.

Early Sunday evening, July 18th, 2021, we received the call from the hospital saying that Molly was not a viable organ or tissue donor. Carson, Ka Hee, and I went back to the hospital to have the hospital turn off the machines. It was a few minutes past 6:00 p.m. when the nursing staff disconnected Molly from life support. The nursing staff told us patients' hearts stop beating quickly, five minutes, ten at the most. Finally, 34 minutes later, Molly passed. That whole time I wondered, did we make a mistake? Her heart kept beating for 34 minutes!

I did not ask Bethlehem Evangelical Lutheran Church, where we still had membership, to do the funeral. I asked Epiphany Lutheran Church, a Missouri Synod church where we were regularly attending, to perform the funeral service. Epiphany treated us as members and extended all the benefits of membership, including bringing meals to the house for a couple of weeks afterward. Bethlehem did nothing and said nothing about Molly's passing.

The pastor from Bethlehem attended Molly's funeral service at Epiphany. I don't know how he found out. He showed up at the funeral and sat alone in the back. Then he talked to me briefly in the fellowship hall afterward. Later, he came over to me and said, "I spilled coffee in a Missouri Synod Church. I'd better go."

You asshole. I thought. What a crass thing to say.

The parting gift I received from the pastor from Bethlehem was a letter terminating my membership in both Bethany and the Wisconsin Synod Lutheran Synod.

10. OWNERSHIP

Slowly, I'm getting around to explaining the reason I believe I'm still here, seemingly surrounded by guardian angels. It has a lot to do with the franchise I own and my experiences there.

The Cleaning Authority franchise was about four and a half years old when I bought it, and it had 619 customers. Since then, we've grown the office to close to 900 customers two and a half years or so later. Our revenues are up by close to 60 percent compared to when I bought it.

There have been some challenges, however. On Monday, April 26th, 2021, I had to terminate my general manager. He was stealing from the company, and he was falsifying company records. He had inserted himself into the daily close-out process. Before I realized this, I had noticed a few customer checks that were not completed properly. I couldn't deposit these checks until the customer corrected them. I'd asked the operations manager, "Can you fix this, please?" But the general manager at the time had quickly volunteered to jump in and fix everything.

At first, I thought, OK, that's nice. But then I realized that he was using his new position as the reviewer of the daily close-outs to steal the cash. He removed cash from the deposits on the daily close-out, went into the customer accounts on the system, removed the payment from their account, and issued them a credit. It wasn't until I looked at a report called the Customer Adjustments report that I could see this going on.

I reached out to corporate and asked, "Can you pull system logs for me, tell me how long this has gone on, and help confirm that it's him?" At the corporate, they could see his login credentials, where he removed the customer payment and issued a credit, all within a minute or two. It happened very quickly, over and over again.

Once I had gathered the facts, I worked it out with my operations manager and assistant manager at the time to make sure they were comfortable stepping up to a much more significant role in running the business. They said they had run the company before and assured me they could do that. I told them what was going to happen and prepared the paperwork.

Monday mornings, we have weekly management meetings. When everyone gathered for this Monday meeting, I said, "I had a hard time believing this was happening. I hoped it wasn't happening, but I investigated thoroughly." I turned to this general manager and said, "You've been stealing from the company. You've been falsifying company records." He tried denying it at first, but it was clear.

"You have two options," I said. "One, you resign immediately. Two, I terminate you for fraud, falsification of company records, and theft. And I have not decided whether I will involve the police." He kept trying to deny that he had done it. So, I picked up my pen and slowly started signing the termination letter. He quickly grabbed the resignation letter, signed it, and gave it to me.

I looked him straight in the eyes. "Get your stuff, return the keys. Get out. We don't want to hear from you again."

Mirian, my Assistant Manager, and Erica, my Operations Manager, sat there, stunned. They had a look on their faces as if a bomb had gone off in the room. Even though I'd tried to prepare them ahead of time, they were stunned when I terminated my general manager. I immediately promoted Erica to General Manager and Mirian to Operations Manager. I also gave them a massive bump in pay. But that was one bad egg within an amazing community of humble, hardworking staff, who've had to fight for everything they ever got in life.

As far as growing the business is concerned, we've increased prices along the way. The previous owner had underpriced many customers to try to grow rapidly. It's difficult to clean properly and make money at such ridiculously low prices. We track a variety of metrics to know if we are pricing our work correctly based on market conditions and on what it costs to send a team out to clean. We calculate drive time, mileage, supplies, insurance, time in the house, and company overhead. Overhead includes unemployment insurance and operating expenses, manager salaries, and something to me as the owner.

As I write this, depending on the day, we are sending 22 or 23 teams out to clean and are training several people. Typically, teams are two unless they are training. Training teams have three people. In recent weeks, our weekly payrolls include 54 to 56 people, five of which are on the management team, and one of them is me.

Our office suite includes four offices—one we use as a supply room, a break room-conference room, restrooms, and an oversized, double-bay garage with a loading dock where our dumpster sits. We are able to open that garage door and shovel large heavy things right out the door into the dumpster, very convenient.

The other garage door has a ramp where vehicles can drive into and out of the garage. The garage houses our laundry equipment, and the individual cleaner cubbies—units that each team uses to store their cleaning equipment and supplies. We replaced the old cubbies with new ones as the old ones were poorly made and were falling apart.

Each cleaner cubbie has a place for their upright vacuum and shelves for their hand-held vacuum, and their tote trays that carry cleaning chemicals in six to eight 20-ounce spray bottles, sponges, brushes, scrubbers, and other cleaning tools.

Each team carries a large nylon bag, branded with The Cleaning Authority logo, that is filled with the clean rags, mops, and dusters, called "woolies." Each team puts their dirty cleaning rags, mops, and sponges into garbage bags—they are wet and heavy and soak through the nylon bags. Additionally, each team carries a bucket and a step stool with them to each house they clean.

I'm working diligently to create a culture where the cleaners feel cared about and have the equipment and supplies they need to do their jobs. I want them to feel proud working for my Cleaning Authority office. While pride and feeling cared about is not something we can easily measure, it shows up each day in the energy these people bring with them to work.

Our big 2021 project was replacing and upgrading all equipment, furniture, and supplies used by the teams and the business. Our big 2022 project was setting up a proper network with a firewall, putting new computers and monitors on each desk. We secured our own domain name so we can have business email addresses.

Inside the offices, I worked from the walls outward. If the room needed painting, I called the painter, then I hung whiteboards, and then I installed file cabinets. When we put the file cabinets in place, we didn't have to climb over them to hang the whiteboards, and we didn't have dust coming down behind them. I continued working inward until each office was repainted and refurnished.

"Well, how do you know they'll fit?" Mirian, my assistant manager, kept asking about the files.

"I've been measuring," I said. "We know exactly how big the file cabinets are."

When I slid the first file cabinets in place, the managers all said, "Wow, it all fits just right."

"That's the power of this thing called a tape measure," I said.

* * *

So, here is my plan! I am selling my Cleaning Authority Franchise to my managers over the next eight years. Why? Because they deserve it, and because they are the ones who have made it a success. I explained to my managers that I need them to manage the business and care about it as if they were the owners. I ask them to do it because much of the time I am not able to do it myself. I told them about my medical conditions and my chronic illnesses.

I also showed them pictures that I had on my phone of the medications and medical supplies I use and how it looks when I have the infusion needles inserted into my belly during an infusion. I explained at a high level what my problems are and the weekly regimen I follow for treatment. I also explained that there are times when I have brain fog and fatigue, and I find it difficult to concentrate and focus. People tend to forget that I'm sick. I don't have the outward visible signs of disability; therefore, it's easy to assume that everything's normal with me when it is far from normal.

"So," I said to my managers, "I need you to care about this company as if you own it. Take care of it the way an owner would, and as my thank you to you is it will be your company."

All five managers are participating in purchasing my Cleaning Authority franchise. Two of my managers felt unsure about what I was offering but made a last-minute decision to join in the buy-out. We created a plan and the legal documents to transfer my company to my managers over the next eight years. My managers purchased the first 10 percent on November 1, 2022. Going forward, they will buy 10% every two years until the managers own 40% of the company. Once they own 40% of the company, I asked them to seek an SBA-backed loan from a bank to purchase the remaining 60%. They need to own a minimum amount of equity before a bank will give them a loan to buy the rest of my company. They'll have a much easier time obtaining that loan if they own 30 to

40 percent of the company. While it is not required, it does make the process much easier.

I told them I need income for a while but not forever, and they need time to prepare to take over ownership of the company. The only significance to starting the process in the Fall of 2022 was that two years after I bought the franchise, we could finish the legal documents without rushing. I know they will never regret purchasing this company from me.

Patty at first said she wasn't sure and had to talk to her husband. He told her, "If you don't say yes, I'm saying yes." She came back and said, "I'm definitely a yes." Julissa was not sure how she felt about participating, but did call me on a Sunday afternoon before we signed the paperwork to ask questions and to say she wanted to participate. At the tender age of 25, she already owns part of a company.

Effective November 1st, 2022, my managers purchased the first 10% of my company. We gathered on a Saturday morning at a UPS store where we all signed the documents and had them notarized. I gave each manager a welcome card, and an expensive bottle of champagne, and took them and their families out to a very nice celebratory lunch.

When I bought the Cleaning Authority business, I looked around at my staff and thought people who grew up in the United States and enjoy all of the privileges of living there have no idea what these people have been through. Many Americans have no appreciation of how hard these peoples' lives have been and how hard they have worked to be able to come to the United States for the opportunity to improve their lives. I realized that the heart and soul of the business are the people that work there, and I learned that every one of them has a story of hardship to tell.

Erica is a DACA child. At age nine, she came with her family to the United States from Puebla, Mexico, outside of Mexico City. She is caught up in the whole situation with the Deferred Action for Childhood Arrivals program and has to redo paperwork every two years to be able to stay in the United States and work here legally. Mirian and her family officially received asylum in February 2021. She's from Maracaibo, Venezuela. It is a beautiful country. I've seen pictures of the house they had to abandon when they left their country because things are so horrible there. They are highly educated people; her husband Ernesto worked as an engineer in the oil industry in Venezuela. They left everything and came here. She started working as a cleaner, then got promoted to manager, and I've continued to promote her ever since.

11. LEADERSHIP

We had a big party for Mirian when she officially received asylum. I found out about it on a February morning in 2021. I went to Staples and had a 4'x6' banner made to congratulate her and her family. I bought cakes and supplies for an office party.

That was the same day that Mirian was planning to surprise her kids, who had been begging her for a dog. She got this little puffball of a dog and called it Luna. She had all the dog equipment—the carrying cage and everything—and she set up the cage at the office at the end of the day because she was going to wrap it to surprise the kids.

Mirian had bought a lot of extra wrapping paper but still managed to wrap the cage in such a way that she ran out of wrapping paper and the carrier was not completely wrapped. Erica teased her, "I don't know how you do that. You even bought extra wrapping paper, and you still ran out." The door to the dog carrier was only partially wrapped. Her solution was to hide the dog in the cage outside on the front step while the kids searched the house, looking for the surprise. I said, "Mirian, it's 10 degrees out there. You're going to have a pupsicle if you're not careful." She caught the pun.

That night, she sent me a picture. She had taken the banner home and hung it above the sofa. In the picture, the whole family was there on the sofa, including the new addition, Luna. Everyone looked so happy, so grateful, so thankful. It melted my heart. I was able to in some small way contribute.

* * *

I stopped a number of the practices that the prior owner was doing. When he became upset with the cleaners, he would take away the houses they were cleaning, and then they had no work for the day. I thought, we don't behave that way. We behave as adults.

If somebody needs to be told something, we pull them off to the side and talk to them about what we want to do for our customers and how we want things to be. If somebody's being negative and poisoning the environment, we take them off to the side and talk to them about that.

I told the managers I wanted us as leaders to use positive language. Instead of saying, "Don't do this, don't do that," we can flip it around and say, "You can do this," and "please do the following."

We run a rewards program for one month each year called Employee Appreciation Month. The cleaners leave a half sheet of paper with their names on it that says, "Do you love your cleaning? Please let us know. If you leave a Google review for us and mention our names, we earn a bonus."

Each time there is a good review for Employee Appreciation Month, it's a review for the team, and every review is worth a $50 bonus. Each member of the team receives $25. In 2021, I paid $4,150 in bonus money. In 2022, I paid $5,250 in bonus money. I told everybody, "Please let us know if you don't want cash; Mirian and Julissa would be pleased to take the cash off your hands." Then I called out names, starting with the lowest bonuses. In 2022, finally, we got to Delmi and Leti. I had the last two envelopes in my hand, and Mirian had a small one that pops open when the attached cord is pulled, and it blasts confetti high into the air. Leti and Delmi each earned $525 in bonus money. We all celebrated everyone's achievements.

I've hired the Language Training Center to help my managers improve their English. My goal is to not only help them on the job but to help them for the rest of their lives. I have a quote on my wall from Jerry Rice: "Today, I will do what others won't. So tomorrow, I can do what others can't." I had that translated into Spanish and hung a copy in each manager's office.

The office is one hundred percent Spanish-speaking, and I am working to improve my Spanish language skills. We try to celebrate everyone's culture in a number of ways. The prior owner had four or five country flags hung on the break room wall. I looked around and said, "First, we're not respecting these people and their cultures." Some flags were stained and spattered by things splashing in the sink. And we didn't have flags for everybody who worked there.

Over time, I ensured that we had a flag for everyone's country. We hung them on the walls in the entranceway and the main hallway until I found the proper mounting hardware and stands. When I finally found bases and mounting hardware, I had a local machine shop manufacture the flag poles from aluminum stock. The flags all now stand on seven-foot poles. Each manager has their flag by their desk, and the front entranceway looks like the United Nations. It's very colorful.

We now have 14 flags in our front entranceway. The last flag I put up was mine, the German flag. It sticks out in the middle of a sea of flags from Spanish-speaking countries and the U.S. flag. At first, it caused a bit of a stir, because the German flag has a broad black stripe on the top. Everybody said, "Oh, that's really different." All the flags from South America are colorful and bright; none feature black like that.

We also have a motto at work, which we borrowed from the license plates in Quebec and modified slightly. I'd traveled to Montreal and noticed the license plates say, Je me souviens. That translates as "I remember." I asked people walking around on the street, "Why do the license plates say that? What does that mean?" People gave me an answer that I loved. It means, basically, "I remember my culture, my heritage, my history, and my language." I thought, oh, I like that.

I created a banner to hang above the flags, with the phrase translated into Spanish: "We remember our culture, our heritage, our history, and our language."

When I commented to corporate headquarters that the front entranceway looked like the United Nations, the corporate staff immediately wanted pictures. I snapped some pictures with my phone. I sent the pictures to them along with a brief explanation, all of which landed in the next Cleaning Authority newsletter.

* * *

I keep reminding the managers to work on themselves; to do something to improve themselves each day, and that in time, they'll find that they're in a place completely different from the people who did nothing to improve themselves. These are things I've tried to teach everyone in the company.

For example, I emphasize why we need insurance. Insurance is for the big emergencies in your life. I keep saying that if you don't have insurance, please do yourself a favor and sign up for insurance. Because if and when you have a significant emergency, you will be glad you have it.

I point out that the two and a half days from when Molly collapsed in the house, around five o'clock on Thursday, July 15th, until she was pronounced dead in the hospital, midday on Sunday, cost about $132,000. Fortunately, I had to pay very little of that because insurance paid for almost everything.

I keep encouraging people to live a life where they are not living from paycheck to paycheck. Many people think I got paid, and it's Friday. I'm good for another week. It's critical to be able to think beyond that.

I've been planning and working on goals for many years, and I'm now in a position where I've seen many of them come to fruition. I own a successful, growing business, and I've been able to invest in real estate as security for my future. My real estate will go to my children, and the business is being purchased by my managers over time. Everyone can find their path in life.

So, after so many close calls, a rough childhood, a whirlwind financial career, the loss of my wife, and debilitating health issues, what I'm finding is that I've got close to 60 people working for me from 14 central and South American countries. These people have given up their culture, their heritage, their history, their language to come here in search of a better life, and they're not always treated very well. So perhaps, the very reason I am still here is to lift them up and to help them.

The management team now owns 10 percent of the company, and they'll continue to buy the company in 10 percent increments. I never said it was free, but what I am doing for them is acting as a bank and removing the need for them to save for years until they finally have enough for a down payment. The managers will become owners decades sooner than if they had to do it in thc traditional way, which is to build a credit history, save a down payment, and borrow from a bank to finally make the purchase.

I have asked the managers to do one thing when they own 40 percent of my company, which is a big chunk of the pie. I have asked them to first go to the bank and ask for a loan to purchase the remaining 60 percent. If for some reason the bank refuses to give them a loan, I have promised to be the bank one last time and to finance them so that they can buy the remaining 60 percent.

Our entranceway with our logo, the 14 country flags (for the countries of our staff), and our banner above the flags.

Our 14 country flags and our banner that says: "We remember our culture, our heritage, our history, and our language."

My entire staff, cleaners and managers, with me in front of the country flags in our entranceway.

My managers with me in front of the country flags in our entranceway.

My managers with me in front of the staff picture wall in the breakroom.

Aracely Ramos, my manager and inspector. She is from San Salvador, El Salvador.

Patricia Lopez, my manager and inspector. She is from Oaxaca, Mexico.

Julissa Garcia, my assistant manager and estimator. She is from Zacatecas, Mexico.

Mirian Machado, my operations manager. She is from Maracaibo, Venezuela.

Erika Santamaria, my general manager. She is from Puebla, Mexico.

I am the owner, and a second-generation German, from Fort Atkinson, Wisconsin.

EPILOGUE

After the night of the email from the Chief Operating Officer of The Authority Brands conglomerate, the night when I went to bed and said a prayer, I got up the next morning and robotically got myself ready for work. I always showered and dressed, even when working from home. It put me in a better frame of mind. I was still sick to my stomach and absorbed in circular thoughts as I tried to think what my COO wanted to meet about.

I couldn't eat, but coffee seemed a good idea, as long as it didn't bring on a sweat. Scratch that, I realized the shower had already been a waste of time as beads formed on my forehead. I fell into a morose state, convinced that I was going to be fired, or worse, my franchise dissolved. What would happen to my staff? My commitment? My purpose?

I arranged my desk neatly. It was always neat, so this was fruitless. I looked out the window and pondered what I would do if I was home all day without a job. Write a book? Travel? Adopt a dog? Who would I talk to? What problems would I solve?

I sat down and prepared to join the meeting.

Microsoft Teams launched. It was 8:44 am. I was in the waiting room. 8:45, 8:46…I contemplated reading some news on my phone, but I was afraid it would destabilize my thoughts.

Ping. That ominous sound that informs you someone has let you into the meeting.

"Good morning, Todd!" boomed the COO. I had noticed that lots of people think they have to shout when communicating over digital airways.

Then, I saw the three other VPs that were attending—marketing, human resources, and media. Oh, I'm fucked, I thought.

"Congratulations!" I thought I heard the COO say.

If I wasn't in a state of paralysis before, I certainly was now.

"Congratulations for what?" I asked. And what came next was beyond my comprehension.

Apparently, the C-suite had nominated me for the Franchisee of the Year Award for Diversity and Inclusion. It was a national award, and I had won.

* * *

I had won the Franchisee of the Year Award from the International Franchise Association, an organization of more than 1,400 franchisor companies, such as the Authority Brands with its 14 franchise brands and hundreds of franchisee offices. It was an accomplishment that meant more to me than any profitable asset maneuvers or investment fund. This was the culmination of a team effort to respect and include people in a positive endeavor. It cemented my thoughts that what I was doing was the right thing and meant a lot to many deserving people.

I attended the franchise award events from February 28th through March 1st, 2022, in San Diego. I had one special request that I hoped the hotel could accommodate and my work would pay for. I asked my COO if the company could arrange to have distilled water in my hotel room. Every other time I'd traveled, I'd always had to trek across town and find someplace I could buy distilled water when I arrived, which was a hassle. While staying in a hotel, you don't know where anything is in town. You've been traveling all day. You drop your bags in the room and think, OK, before I can relax. I've got to find distilled water.

"Todd," my COO said. "You can have anything you like. As far as I'm concerned, you're golden."

* * *

After the ceremony, I brought the award to the office to share with everyone. We keep it on the photo shelves with pictures of all the teams who work there—it's a semi-circular, glass plaque about a half-inch thick with an engraving of the business name and "International Franchise Association, Franchisee of the Year."

Of all my work-related efforts, receiving this award has been the most gratifying. But it's only there because everybody had a hand in making it possible.

CLOSING

If someone claims to be a self-made success, the truth is more likely to be that they had lots of help along the way.

I have described some alternative and non-traditional paths that I have walked and those who I know have taken. In my case, they included a difficult childhood, walking away from myriad accidents, a confusing education, a thrilling ride through corporate America, a risky approach to investing, and unconventional leadership. I've also described a lifelong challenge with my health. Still, despite all that, it's all turned out alright.

I now believe that guardian angels looked after me all those years so that I could pay something forward. Whether or not that's true doesn't really matter, because I feel more fulfilled than I ever have in my life. All my experiences have taught me something. It's very easy to become proud and to assume that we and we alone achieve whatever it is that we accomplish, but the truth is, every one of us is where we are thanks to a lot of help from the people around us.

I was a guest on a podcast with an entrepreneur named Tim Campsall, who does a series called "Self-Made is a

Myth." Campsall says that if someone claims to be a self-made success, the truth is they had lots of help along the way.

In my case, this really applies. I have help every week from thousands of people willing to walk into plasma centers and provide plasma so that I can function as well as I do. Plus, there's all the help I've had from mentors and partners in business and life. And now, I have the help of my team at The Cleaning Authority.

So, whatever you are going through, you can still accomplish your hopes and dreams, but you may have to do it in a non-traditional way. Have belief in others, believe in yourself, and believe that you can achieve what you want. Most importantly, remember that you are never alone.

* * *

My management team was excited when they heard about the Franchisee of the Year award. Erica, who shares the front office with me, ran down the hall to tell the other managers. I could hear them all cheering and clapping. Next, they started calling me Chingón. At first, I wasn't sure what the heck that was, so I asked.

"Badass," they said.

My 2016 Acura TLX that I very much enjoy driving.

I am waving from the driver's seat of my Acura.

StoryTerrace